AF324868

TIME'S GLORY

Original Essays

on

ROBERT PENN WARREN

edited by

James A. Grimshaw, Jr.

Associate Editors

Cleanth Brooks
Albert Erskine
James Justus
Richard Law
Lewis Simpson

Editorial Assistant

Blaize A. Stewart

General Editor

Robert E. Lowrey

University of Central Arkansas Press

1986

Cover Art and Illustrations - Robert Lowrey

Library of Congress Cataloging in Publication Data

Time's Glory.
Bibliography: p. 119
1. Warren, Robert, Penn, 1905- -Criticism and interpretation. I. Grimshaw, James A.
PS3545.A748Z89 1986 813'.52 86-25015

ISBN 0-9615143-2-9

Manufactured in the United States of America

To

My Parents

Maurine Haley Grimshaw

and

James A. Grimshaw, Sr.

"Time's glory is to calm contending kings,
To unmask falsehood, and bring truth to light,
To stamp the seal of time in aged things,
To wake the morn, and sentinel the night,
To wrong the wronger till he render right,
    To ruinate proud buildings with thy hours,
    And smear with dust their glitt'ring golden towers;

"To fill with worm-holes stately monuments,
To feed oblivion with decay of things,
To blot old books, and alter their contents,
To pluck the quills from ancient ravens' wings,
To dry the old oak's sap, and cherish springs,
    To spoil antiquities of hammer'd steel,
    And turn the giddy round of Fortune's wheel;

"To show the beldam daughters of her daughter,
To make the child a man, the man a child,
To slay the tiger that doth live by slaughter,
To tame the unicorn and lion wild,
To mock the subtle in themselves beguil'd,
    To cheer the ploughman with increaseful crops,
    And waste huge stones with little water-drops."

– *The Rape of Lucrece*

CONTENTS

PREFACE

The seven original essays contained in this collection represent the continuing interest in and reassessment of all facets of Robert Penn Warren's canon. They are only a portion of the manuscripts submitted in response to the "call for papers" in the fall of 1985. At that time the selected manuscripts were to have been included in a special issue of the *Publications of the Arkansas Philological Association* (*PAPA*), a journal edited at the University of Central Arkansas. Plans escalated, however, and the editor of *PAPA* decided that the author, about whom the essays are written, warranted a more visible, permanent recognition. This book is a result of that decision.

A panel of five judges read the initial submissions and recommended publication of the best of them. The judges, Cleanth Brooks, Albert Erskine, James Justus, Richard Law, and Lewis Simpson, read the manuscripts without knowing the identity of the writers. After their selections were made, I asked the judges for contributions if their schedules permitted. Therefore, these essays were judged on their merits rather than on the reputation of their authors. Procedures notwithstanding, it should not surprise readers of this volume that most of the contributors are, indeed, well-known in Warren studies.

Such a random process leads inevitably to an unbalanced collection: five essays deal with Warren's fiction, one with his poetry, and one with his nonfiction. What does result from a less orchestrated selection, though, is a richer, more innovative approach to Warren's works. If these essays may be considered representative of the latest in Warren scholarship, then collectively they suggest a more eclectic reading of the entire canon and less of an *explication de texte.* Independently they indicate a reinforcement of the reevaluation of Warren's themes, narrative technique, and uses of history.

Organization of the essays is roughly from the one dealing with the earliest novel, *Night Rider*, to the essay which deals with the later novels. That essay, by Leonard Casper, also draws most heavily among the first five on the interrelatedness between the poetry and the fiction and serves as a transition between the section on fiction and the section on poetry. Victor Strandberg's essay, similarly, serves as a bridge between Casper's concerns and James Justus's treatment of some of Warren's nonfiction. The arrangement, then, is intended to serve as a continuous whole, although each of the pieces stands by the weight of its own premises.

Frances Bixler focuses on the successes and failures of five protagonists to overcome acedia (sloth): Percy Munn in *Night Rider*, Jeremiah Beaumont in *World Enough and Time*, Cassie Killigrew Spottwood in *Meet Me in the Green Glen*, Jack Burden in *All the King's Men*, and Jed Tewksbury in *A Place to Come To*. The protagonists who overcome acedia gain insights which enable them to achieve knowledge which, in time, might lead to their redemption.

William Bedford Clark's essay also traces a single motif through several novels. Clark deals with the secret sharer figures–those blacks who represent *alter egos* and who serve as foils to white protagonists: Brad Tolliver and Jingle Bells in *Flood*, Cassie Spottwood and Arlita in *Meet Me in the Green Glen*, and Jed Tewksbury and Swami in *A Place to Come To*. Clark sees these "secret sharers" not merely as "literary artifices" but as reinforcement of one of Warren's central themes–"we are only ourselves." This realization, too, is a kind of knowledge; and it allows those protagonists who accept it to make peace with themselves and with others.

Although both Richard G. Law and Randolph Runyon deal primarily with one novel, *World Enough and Time* and *The Cave*, respectively, each draws on the depth and breadth of the Warren canon to buttress his claims. Law sees the main thrust of the novel's technique as involving the reader in ferreting out meaning, in making meaning out of action, a technique he feels becomes lost in the Jeremiah Beaumont drama. Noting the irony of contraries (spirit and flesh), Law works out the steps by which Beaumont comes to his final awareness of the commonality of men and the consequences of that awareness. Following that discussion, Law deals with the anticlimactic structure of the novel and its force in light of the pastoral tradition.

Runyon, on the other hand, introduces his "fictive fetus" theory and sees the absent center of *The Cave* as Jack Harrick, the man trapped inside the cave. Blending this central image with other works of Warren, Runyon reads the novel as a more subtle statement by

Warren on the creative process of fiction.

Leonard Casper seems to reinforce Runyon's finding about Warren's creative process and adds to it the ways in which the poetry and fiction coalesce. Casper examines the narrative perspective of the solitary, central characters in *The Cave, Wilderness, Flood, Meet Me in the Green Glen*, and *A Place to Come To*, perspectives which share the view of the "sameness of all men."

Victor Strandberg updates his assessment of Warren as poet and demonstrates how Warren earns the label, "Poet of Youth." Although Strandberg's examination centers on "Altitudes and Extensions" in Warren's new volume of poetry, *New and Selected Poems*, he connects earlier poems with those presented between 1980-1984. Basically, Strandberg justifies Warren's "youthfulness" because Warren returns to boyhood images, develops further the early themes, and in his latest poems writes poems of rejuvenation. The last poem in the latest addition to the canon, "Myth of Mountain Sunrise," Strandberg sees as a "culminating expression of Warren's central themes and images."

Looking at Warren's great generative theme, Time, James Justus explores the bases of the best of Warren's historical writing: factuality, surmise, and memory. Justus discusses at greatest length *The Legacy of the Civil War* and *Jefferson Davis Gets His Citizenship Back*, two works which allow readers to see the commentator as a small boy at his grandfather's knee and as an older man looking back over history and his life.

Rather than combine into one list of works cited each contributor's selected bibliography, I have listed them individually, as an index of the interrelatedness among Warren's works as well as among the larger whole of literature. I have tried to keep editorial meddling to a minimum, adjusting documentation to coincide with the *MLA Style Manual* (1985), adding only one editorial note, and arranging minor stylistic features for the sake of consistency. Such discrepancies, if found, are mine and not the authors' who have provided these provocative readings of Warren's works.

Besides those acknowledged elsewhere in this collection, my sincere thanks goes to James Kempf, Frostburg State College, Maryland, for his continued interest in and suggestions on this project; to James Byrd and Dorys Grover, East Texas State University, for numerous materials on Warren and for their lively discussions about Warren;

and to Keith McFarland, Dean for Graduate Studies and Research at East Texas State University, for his continued support of our scholarly pursuits.

JAGJr

Greenville, Texas
August 10, 1986

Acknowledgments

Grateful acknowledgment is made to Random House, Inc., and the author for permission to quote from the copyrighted material of Robert Penn Warren: *All The King's Men*, copyright 1953 by Random House, Inc.; *At Heaven's Gate*, copyright 1943 by Robert Penn Warren; *Band of Angels*, copyright 1955 by Robert Penn Warren; *Being Here: Poetry 1977-1980*, copyright 1978, 1979, 1980 by Robert Penn Warren; *Brother to Dragons: A Tale in Verse and Voice–A New Version*, copyright 1953, 1979 by Robert Penn Warren; *The Cave*, copyright 1959 by Robert Penn Warren; *Chief Joseph of the Nez Perce*, copyright 1982, 1983 by Robert Penn Warren; *Flood*, copyright 1963, 1964 by Robert Penn Warren; *Homage to Theodore Dreiser*, copyright 1971 by Robert Penn Warren; *The Legacy of the Civil War* copyright 1961 by Robert Penn Warren; *Meet Me in the Green Glen*, copyright 1971 by Robert Penn Warren; *New and Selected Poems, 1923-1985*, copyright 1985 by Robert Penn Warren; *Night Rider*, copyright 1939, copyright renewed 1966 by Robert Penn Warren; *Or Else–Poem/Poems 1968-1974*, copyright 1966, 1968, 1970, 1971, 1972, 1973, 1974 by Robert Penn Warren; *A Place to Come To*, copyright 1977 by Robert Penn Warren; *Rumor Verified: Poems 1979-1980*, copyright 1979, 1980, 1981 by Robert Penn Warren; *Segregation*, copyright 1956 by Robert Penn Warren; *Selected Essays*, copyright 1941, 1943, 1944, 1946, 1947, 1958 by Robert Penn Warren; *Selected Poems: New and Old, 1923-1966*, copyright 1966 by Robert Penn Warren; *Selected Poems, 1923-1975*, copyright 1976 by Robert Penn Warren; *Selected Poems of Herman Melville*, copyright 1967, 1970 by Robert Penn Warren; *Who Speaks for the Negro?*, copyright 1965 by Robert Penn Warren; *Wilderness*, copyright 1961 by Robert Penn Warren; *World Enough and Time*, copyright 1950 by Robert Penn Warren; *You, Emperors, and Others: Poems 1957-1960*, copyright 1958, 1959, 1960 by Robert Penn Warren; and from *Robert Penn Warren Talking: Interviews 1950-1978*, copyright 1980 by Random House, Inc.

Preparation of this manuscript was made possible, in part, by a grant from the Faculty Research Fund, East Texas State University and the expert skills of data processor Ann Martin.

THE FICTION

Acedia: The Most Deadly Sin in Robert Penn Warren's Fictive World

Frances Bixler

Since the early part of this century, artists have been portraying the spiritual decay of our times. "The best lack all conviction," W. B. Yeats declares in "The Second Coming." In his vision, Western society lacks the will to pursue good, ensuring that a new era is about to begin. Central to Yeats's nightmare vision is the "rough beast" which "slouches" to its birthplace. "Slouches" suggests the inertia inherent in this new society which will be known for its bestial nature.

Robert Penn Warren fleshes out Yeats's nightmare vision in his novels. Characters like Dr. MacDonald, Professor Ball, Murray Guilfort, Bogan Murdock, Willie Stark, Wilkie Barron, and Ikie Sumpter are bestial men who suck the life out of society for their own selfish purposes. They are the people of "passionate intensity" who have given themselves over completely to unreality and evil. Others like Willie Proudfit, Ashby Wyndham, Leroy Lancaster, Cass Mastern, and Elvira Simms have a vision of the good and a clear picture of their own potential for evil; and they spend their energy in pursuit of their vision. They have "seen the light," as Ashby Wyndham would say, and have determined to follow it. Warren casts these people as supporting actors in the larger drama of his fictive world which focuses on the characters who are not yet completely devoted to either good or evil but are struggling to define themselves in a world where the signs have become blurred or lost and the temptation to give way to acedia beckons powerfully.

Such a struggle is not new. Dante addresses the problem when he places acedia in the center cornice of *The Purgatorio*, halfway up the mountain, halfway through his journey, and central to the meaning of his quest. For the medieval person, the sin of acedia was a sin which could damn one's soul to hell because it created the environment which enabled one to accept both evil and good unthinkingly. Dante gives examples of characters who throw off acedia: "Mary *ran* to the hills" . . . "Caesar, to subdue Ilerda struck at Marseilles, and then *swooped* down on Spain" (18.100-02). Action verbs indicate the posture necessary for spiritual health. Dante follows up with examples of characters who fail to throw off their lethargy: the children of Israel's lack of zeal doomed their prospects for living in the Promised Land, and Aeneas was forced to leave several people behind in Sicily because they did not want to share the risks of founding Rome. Dante himself has given in to acedia; his journey is the necessary antidote. John Ciardi's note on acedia (sloth) as Dante perceived it is instructive:

> Sloth must not be understood as physical laziness or slovenliness but as torpor of the soul which, loving the good, does not pursue it actively enough. . . .
>
> Acedia, however, is not simply the failure to perform good works for others, though it readily involves that failure. It is, more specifically, the failure to pay enough attention to the good, to make enough demands upon oneself. . . . Acedia may consist in being too torpid to arrive at a vision of the good, or in achieving that vision but neglecting to pursue it. (*Purgatorio* 185)

Warren's fictive world contains characters who possess some or all of these traits. In particular, I would like to focus on five central characters who demonstrate Warren's consistent attempt to present acedia as the most pervasive modern failing.[1]

Three central characters fail in their attempt to throw off their "torpor of soul." Percy Munn's struggle against himself shows the destructive power of acedia. At the beginning of *Night Rider*, Percy is caught in the center of a mass of people whose movements are dictated by the jerky braking of the train. This initial image has been interpreted by some as proof of Warren's naturalistic vision of man.[2] In light of Warren's later works, however, the image more accurately suggests the way Percy thinks of himself. He does not consider himself separate and capable of acting on his own, nor does he struggle against being shoved this way and knocked that way. He merely registers discontent as the crowd limits his vision and makes his decisions.

Percy's story supports this initial image. Swayed by his inner need to defend the good (and also to win a hopeless case), Percy exposes his weakness when he willingly falls in with Bunk Trevalyan's plot to frame a helpless black man for his murder. This early struggle suggests that Percy has a vision of the good and wishes to devote himself to energetically defending it, but no further action in the story indicates that such is true.[3] When Percy is asked to join the Association, he is flattered by the attention of the older, more powerful men. Warren rarely shows him struggling with the ethical problems of a society like the Association. Instead, Percy seems simply to drift into the deeper and deeper mire of the notion that the end justifies the means. Even more revealing is Percy's willingness to join a group like the Brotherhood which is founded on the principle of violence. He swears "I, Percy Munn, . . . will steadfastly support the purpose of the . . . Brotherhood . . . and whatever measures may be deemed advisable for the accomplishment of that purpose–and . . . I will loyally obey the commands of the truly elected officers superior to me in this organization . . ." (155-56). His oath releases him from thinking for himself, from taking initiative, and from guilt. Willingly Percy swears fealty to a force which is out of control. Raking a neighbor's plant beds, burning a friend's barn, killing a man, committing adultery with a friend's only daughter, violating his wife–all these actions are possible for Percy because he has ceased to struggle against the spiritual malaise which disguises his misdeeds as work for the good.

The depth of his lethargy becomes apparent at the end of the novel when he hides at Willie Proudfit's farm, unable to make order out of his experiences and unwilling to face his own wrongdoing. His vision of May holding the baby wrapped in newspaper–a baby with a face like Bunk Trevalyan–symbolizes the nature of Percy's actions. His "torpor of soul" has fathered evil. Percy's physical death only completes the spiritual death which has already taken place much earlier in the novel.

Like Munn, Jeremiah Beaumont also swears fealty to the idea of Justice; but his struggle takes on different dimensions. Always Jeremiah seems to have been a struggler, a seeker after something which will give his life integrity. His early religious experiences indicate that he longs for the insight which will give meaning to his life. When he is drawn by Wilkie Barron into Rachael Jordan's tragedy, he gradually comes to believe that defending Justice–which in practical terms means killing Fort–is the act which will give his life the yearned-for order. People, Jeremiah firmly believes, should always do the right thing; and if they do not, some perfect person should see that they are punished. He, of course, is the perfect person in this case. Thus, he determines to kill Cassius Fort. Also like Percy Munn, Jeremiah does his best to cover his wrongdoing with a patina of goodness. He can thus persuade himself that by murdering his mentor and friend he is cleansing the world of an unjust man. The reader sees the irony in his position. How does a murder justify adultery? Yet Jeremiah suffers much anguish before he is able to understand his ethical and moral mistake.

Basically, Jeremiah's problem is that he separates "being" from "doing." His story would have run much differently if he had said to himself, "I must not just defend Justice; I must *be* just." A just man is able to recognize and accept responsibility for his crimes against humanity and against himself. After much suffering and a period of complete acedia in the swamps of the Gran Boz, Jeremiah admits painfully that he is guilty of murder, of using Rachael for his own satisfaction, of willing his mother's death, of hitting Wilkie out of hurt pride, of participating in politics for his own need, of deceiving Madison and Hawgood, of manipulating Dr. Burnham, and, finally, of being himself (458). And we might add that he is guilty of failing to wrestle with the conflicting values in his life. In the end, Jeremiah's struggle becomes his defeat. Too late he comes to the realization that the self is not "something you go find under a leaf. The self is what you *do*. What you want to do, and what you do do" (*Talking* 296). Warren succinctly judges his own character when he says:

> Man must make his life somehow in the dialectical process of these terms [the paradoxes of human existence], and insofar as he is to achieve redemption he must do so through an awareness of his condition, not in abstraction, not in mere doctrine, but immediately. ("The Great Mirage" 54)

Jeremiah's unwillingness to *do* good results in his inability to "achieve redemption." He does end his life much wiser than Percy Munn, however, who dies without any knowledge of his own culpability.

Cassie Killigrew is a central character in *Meet Me in the Green Glen* whose pitiful struggle against the larger society suggests that she is a victim, not an actor; but Cassie is only a victim of her own acedia. Her special variety of acedia is that of withdrawal. After her great disappointment when Cy Grinder walks out of her hospital room without looking back, Cassie limits her real world to that which goes on inside her head. In the sixteen years of her marriage to Sunderland Spottwood, she grows increasingly skillful in ducking out of the too-painful reality of this world. The novel opens with Cassie's deliberating over whether the man she sees walking down the road is a figment of her imagination or a real person. She has so successfully drawn into herself that only with great effort can she make these distinctions.

Cassie rarely struggles to separate reality from nonreality, truth from nontruth. Hence, she calls herself Mrs. Spottwood and accepts the duties of being Sunder's wife, but she never faces up to her real feelings which cause Sunder to describe her as "bottled up." At her mother's funeral she is not able to cry even though she has a terrible need to do so. Instead, she opts for the nonreality of an emotional breakdown. When Murray Guilfort offers her money, Cassie mutely accepts it, never questioning his motives or his need to dominate her. Later, when Angelo brings home the red ribbon, the red nail polish, and the red dress, she thinks of herself as beautiful though Angelo is debasing her into a common streetwalker.

It is this lack of practice in distinguishing between issues which makes it impossible for Cassie to become suddenly strong in defending the truth. Unlike Munn and Jeremiah, she makes public confession of her wrongdoing in the dramatic scene in the courtroom when Angelo is pronounced guilty of Sunder's murder. The society around her, however, is not supportive of these, her first responsible steps toward goodness. They persist in believing the lie which Murray has so convincingly managed. Too late Cassie learns that "salvation–real existence–comes only with a commitment to others, a sharing in the human communion, a sense that all human actions are intricately interrelated" (Guttenberg 131). Her continuing struggle to be believed results in Leroy Lancaster's redemption, but Cassie can do nothing to save Angelo. Nor, finally, can she save herself. Her habit of slipping into the acedia of withdrawal overtakes her, and she returns to the mental hospital to live out her days in nonreality.

Two of Warren's characters struggle successfully against their spiritual lethargy. The first is Jack Burden who, after spending most of his adult life indulging in the "Great Sleep" or believing in the

"Great Twitch" theory, comes to the realization that he must participate in the commonness of humanity and thus become a responsible human being. Jack is a long time resisting such a commitment. After he discovers that Anne Stanton has become the mistress of Willie Stark, he flees westward where he discovers his "dream," which he calls "bracing and tonic." In reality it is just another defense mechanism he has erected against the truth:

> At first it was, as I have said, rather bracing and tonic. For after the dream there is no reason why you should not go back and face the fact which you have fled from . . . for any place to which you may flee will not be like the place from which you have fled, and you might as well go back, after all, to the place where you belong, for nothing was your fault or anybody's fault, for things are always as they are. And you can go back in good spirits, for you will have learned two very great truths. First, that you cannot lose what you have never had. Second, that you are never guilty of a crime which you did not commit. (311)

A better definition of acedia would be hard to find. In his refusal to admit his complicity in Anne's decision to go to Willie Stark, Jack denies that he belongs to any community or carries any responsibility for anyone; he plans only to drift. Though he is far more active in the world than Cassie Killigrew, he, nevertheless, is behaving in similar fashion, ducking the truth. Unlike Cassie, however, Jack has all of his life wrestled with issues involving values; the position he assumes after learning the painful truth about Anne is a temporary refuge from which he emerges later in the novel.

Not until he digs up all the "truth" about Judge Irwin, the Scholarly Attorney, and his mother is Jack jolted into the realization that no one can sneer at and criticize and judge the human community without sneering at and criticizing and judging himself. Jack Burden condemns Jack Burden. His own research has uncovered his own culpability; thus, he accepts his role in the violent deaths of Adam Stanton and Willie Stark and takes his first active steps toward goodness by refusing to tell Sugar Boy about Tiny Duffy's involvement in the double tragedy. His second step is lovingly to accept his mother's feelings and to attempt to see her as a suffering fellow human being. Third, he marries Anne Stanton—a step which indicates that he chooses to build for the future. In his concluding remarks on Warren's work, Justus catches the gist of Jack's final truth: "What the self discovers in its fitful journey toward knowledge is that the 'so damned special' must be completed by the common; the integrity and uniqueness must join in communion, the acknowledgment of continuities in what it means to be human" (325). For Jack "what it means to be human" finally is that he, too, is an imperfect person who must never give up the search for truth or the need for communion. Such a search requires determined, purposeful, and active effort–light years away from Jack's earlier slothful lifestyle.

A second character who successfully fights free of his spiritual lethargy is Jed Tewksbury. Though not a student of history or a member of a Southern aristocratic family like Jack Burden, Jed's characteristic habit of storing away in his memory important events of his life greatly aids him in his journey toward truth. In the character of Jed, Warren represents fully the sudden forward leaps, the infantile regressions, the stagnations, the false moves which characterize a human being's journey toward truth. Jed, like Jack, certainly makes little linear progress toward illumination; yet as the years pass and experience overlays earlier experience, Jed grows out of his tendency to drift and becomes an active pursuer of the good. The fact that he is fifty-eight before he arrives at his moment of illumination testifies to the difficulty of the journey and to his tenacity.

Jed's memory of the way his father died, "holding on to his dong," colors his youth and early manhood and provides an explanation for his reliance on sexual experience as an avenue to meaning. His brief marriage to Agnes Andresen does nothing to deter his belief that in sexual relationships one can find communion. The affair of Nashville and Rozelle Hardcastle puts Jed's belief to the test. Six months in Nashville floating free from any responsibility, existing only in the fantasy world of sex with Rozelle, is a period of acedia comparable to Munn's sojourn on Willie Proudfit's farm, Jeremiah's flight to the nightmare territory of the Gran Boz, Cassie's escape to the mental hospital, and Jack's "Great Sleep." The first three characters' stories end in the depths of acedia; both Jack and Jed emerge from their lethargy wiser and determined to become active once again. Ultimately, Jed realizes that no two people can relate to each other solely on a sexual basis; and he asks Rozelle to marry him. Rozelle, however, needs Jed only as a sexual person and is much afraid of marriage to him.

Though Jed's second marriage is almost as short-lived as his first, he gains a son and learns, for the first time, what it is to love another human being. The passages describing his feelings about Ephraim as a baby and his later yearning to share himself with the boy suggest that Jed is a good father. Thus, though Jed cannot give himself to Dauphine, he does learn the joy of sacrificial living through his experience as father.

Other important events of Jed's life circle around his friendship with Stephan Mostoski and his professional success. Stephan is Jed's first close friend. They enjoy long conversations about the nature of the universe and the realities of life in the twentieth century. Jed is able to open himself to Stephan's criticism, which proves enormously helpful. When Jed tells Stephan about his reluctance to take Ephraim back to Dugton to share his grief over his mother's death, Stephan charges Jed with selfishness and a need to hang on to his solitude. His words create part of the environment which aids Jed in his discovery of truth.

Certainly, Jed's professional success is a part of his journey, though Warren allows Jed to mouth the twentieth-century intellectual's ironic self-denigration. Years of scholarly work on Dante and the works of medieval love poets have left their mark and have given Jed a basis for thought and for comparison with his own life. As the honors roll in and the work becomes a refuge from the pain of life, Jed tells himself that the function of work is just to keep one busy; but his work has done more than occupy his time. It has helped to order his experience. That he is recognized all over the world for his erudition and diligence testifies to the fact that Jed has not given way to acedia in his professional life.

Finally, Jed's most reliable ally in his fight against spiritual lethargy is his mother, Elvira Simms. She senses that Dugton is no place for a young man with Jed's good mind to grow, and she pushes him out into a world where he can. Elvira also knows intuitively that "Miss Pritty-Pants," as she calls Rozelle, will only bring harm to Jed. More important than her warnings and her firm guidance–even to the breaking of his nose–is her own example of sacrificial living. Without complaint Elvira spends her life working in a cannery in order to put no burden on Jed. She possesses the ability to engender good in others as Perk Simms poignantly tells Jed: "She had the sleight. To make a man always feel like a man. . . . Living with a woman like your ma

. . . it is like you was living in a–a dream–and time ain't gone by, the way she could make you feel that everything kept on being the truth" (388). It is Perk's revelation that Elvira has kept Jed's room in readiness and his bed made up for forty-one years in the secret hope that he will come home to see her which finally brings all the fragments of Jed's life into a whole. His letter to Dauphine suggests that he has at last found out an elemental truth about life:

> I ask for your company because it is what I feel myself most deeply craving.
>
> It is not that I cannot stand solitude. Perhaps I stand it all too easily, and have been, far beyond my own knowing, solitary all my life.
>
> I ask for your company for what blessedness it is. But I say also that in it I may learn, even as the light fails, a little of what I need to know. (395)

To share, to learn, to grow, to commune is the blessedness of being human which costs "not less than everything" as T. S. Eliot says.

Warren's canon represents a wide spectrum of characters struggling against various stages and types of acedia with varying degrees of failure and success. Nowhere does Warren suggest that the struggle is easy or ever permanently won. In a conversation with Bill Moyers, he asserts that

> It's a constant struggle. It means trying to inspect the things that shape us, that make us. Once we understand it, we can sometimes do something about it. . . . People look at what made their world tick or made them tick, and they achieve, may achieve, some sense of freedom from mechanical forces. I mean forces of machines, of mechanisms, but forces that have them into machines and give them habits of doing this thing this way and that way. (*Talking* 204)

Warren's skillful portrayal of what makes Percy and Jeremiah and Cassie and Jack and Jed tick may, indeed, help us free ourselves from the habits which make us into little more than machines.

Notes

[1]Warren's other novels also present variations on this problem but not so clearly or powerfully.

[2]Both Steward and Ransom feel that Warren's early work shows strong naturalistic tendencies.

[3]Guttenberg suggests that Munn's major temptation is his quest for the "ideal of Justice" (8). I agree. Like Jeremiah Beaumont, Munn allows the idea of one virtue to dominate his thinking so thoroughly that he loses sight of all other virtues.

Works Cited

Alighieri, Dante. *The Purgatorio.* Trans. John Ciardi. New York: New American Library, 1957.

Guttenberg, Barnett. *Web of Being: The Novels of Robert Penn Warren.* Nashville: Vanderbilt UP, 1975.

Justus, James H. *The Achievement of Robert Penn Warren.* Baton Rouge: Louisiana State UP, 1981.

Ransom, John Crowe. "The Inklings of Original Sin." *Saturday Review of Literature* 20 May 1944: 10-11. Rpt. in *Robert Penn Warren: Critical Perspectives.* Ed. Neil Nakadate. Lexington: UP of Kentucky, 1981. 207-11.

Stewart, Randall. "Dreiser and the Naturalistic Heresy." *Virginia Quarterly Review* 34 (1958): 100-16.

Warren, Robert Penn. *All the King's Men.* 1946. New York: Bantam, 1951.

—. *Meet Me in the Green Glen.* New York: Random, 1971.

—. *Night Rider.* New York: Random, 1939.

—. "*Nostromo.*" *Sewanee Review* 59 (1951): 363-91. Rpt. as "'The Great Mirage': Conrad and *Nostromo.*" *Selected Essays.* New York: Random, 1958. 31-58.

—. *A Place to Come To.* 1977. New York: Dell, 1978.

—. *World Enough and Time.* New York: Random, 1950.

Watkins, Floyd C., and John T. Hiers, eds. *Robert Penn Warren Talking.* New York: Random, 1980.

Warren's *World Enough and Time*: "Et in Arcadia Ego"

Richard G. Law

And ye shall know the truth and the truth shall make you free.

– John 8:32

"How dreadful knowledge of the truth can be when there is no help in truth."

– Teiresias to Oedipus, *Oedipus the King*

Charles Bohner's remark that in *World Enough and Time* we have "the weirdest tale Warren has given us" (91) remains one of the best short descriptions of the novel. Accounting for the strangeness of the book is a difficult task. One senses greater psychological displacement in *World Enough and Time* than in any of Warren's other work, and greater disparity between the ostensible interests of the book and its submerged issues, which are elusive and well disguised.[1] The novel's place in the writer's career has not yet been established–in fact, has hardly been addressed. Yet both chronologically and aesthetically, the novel marks decisively the end of Warren's early phase of development as an artist: after this performance, Warren emerges on a radically different track as a writer. Moreover, the blackness of the darkness of *World Enough and Time* is unprecedented; the novel represents quite the fullest look at the worst in Warren's entire canon. It is tempting to conjecture that the novel also records a personal crisis, a low-water mark of nihilism and despair in mid-life, and that it dramatizes (behind several layers of disguises) a violent leave-taking of earlier commitments. *World Enough and Time* resembles Warren's other work enough that the extent to which it parodies his earlier ideas and mannerisms has been underestimated. On close inspection, however, the novel not only seems to represent a break with the writer's previous work, but to constitute an attack on and a mockery of previously held positions and assumptions, to mark not just his abandonment of agrarianism and his rejection of the Southern past as an image of a redemptive community, but an abjuring of some of his most fundamental aesthetic ideas as well. If the novel does indeed function as a busk, a ritual consignment of formerly valued goods to the flames, it represents Warren's most intriguing performance in any genre.

World Enough and Time is structured as a kind of philosophical detective story, with the narrator (a thin disguise for the writer)[2] attempting to shape into coherent form what can be known or inferred about a series of bloody, melodramatic events from the past—the basic strategy employed again in Warren's next work, *Brother to Dragons*. The role of the narrator/detective/historian is to push the materials towards revelation—toward "Truth."[3] Part of the evidence which the narrator assembles is itself a narrative—an effort by the nineteenth-century protagonist to make sense of his own actions: "exhibit A" is the journal of a condemned man who is similarly seeking the underlying truth of his experience—or, to use Warren's terms, "redemption" through self-definition and "knowledge." These parallel perspectives set in motion a highly self-conscious and self-referential dialectic. The reader is drawn into the same effort of puzzle-solving, and every major element in the novel is similarly aligned to illustrate (and to test) the form-making, meaning-generating activity of the mind. In lining up the consecutive imaginative acts of protagonist, narrator, and reader, all of which are focused on the same baffling questions, Warren implies, as elsewhere in his fiction and poetry, the identity of the artistic and moral imagination. But the most significant fact about this elaborate structure for dramatizing the self- and world-constructing power of the imagination is that it fails, and fails miserably. Neither nineteenth-century protagonist nor modern commentator uncovers the meaning of what Beaumont does; both end with the same unanswerable question: "Was all for naught?"[4]

As a counterpoint to these quests for "truth," the plot of the novel seems designed expressly to frustrate any effort to obtain insight. The action illustrates (redundantly) the "doubleness" of Jeremiah Beaumont's experience, both in regard to his dualistic frame of reference and to a seemingly ingrained "duplicity" in events. Events are never what they appear; conclusions do not flow from intentions; and nothing has a single significance. Moreover, the narrative pursues (with an almost compulsive tenacity) every hopeful premise of the protagonist to its disastrous conclusion. Through the lenses provided by the impotent modern commentator, the reader follows the erratic course of Jeremiah Beaumont as the action gradually cancels out possible resolution after possible resolution, until he arrives at an ultimate *reductum ad absurdum.* Such a plot is a kind of commentary in itself, especially as we recall that Warren's artistic credo has always affirmed the identity of artistic form and meaning and implied that the form of the work and the perceptive gestalt of the mind are closely analogous, if not identical. The action of *World Enough and Time*, however, appears to take that notion and plunge it into an acid bath. As Robert B. Heilman has pointed out, the novel's total effect "is one of a manically exhaustive ripping apart of excuses, justifications, defenses, ruses, consolations; of a furious burrowing into ever-deeper layers of self-understanding until almost every clarity becomes a puzzle and every dependability a delusion" (98).

I

The protagonist, we are told, is in a sense an artist, and his *magnum opus* is his own life, an "ambiguous drama," scripted with himself in a heroic role.[5] The inconsistencies of his own inner drama eventually drive him to write—and thus to compose consciously—a commentary on the drama which was his life. That act of interpretation superimposed upon his unconscious dramatic script is an attempt to untangle "truth" from illusion and to arrive at a stable version of events and a clear sense of self. The narrative, in turn, consists of a modern historian sifting through the surviving facts in an effort to come to terms with Beaumont's story. The modern commentator/narrator, like Jack Burden, is shown pondering the surviving data of the past—in this case, the scraps of paper, the documents, the crayon portrait, and so on, which are the remains of the Beaumont tragedy. "I can show you what is left," the narrator asserts in the first words of the novel:

> We have what is left, the lies and half-lies and the truths and half-truths. We do not know that we have the Truth. But we must have it. Puzzling over what is left, we are like the scientist fumbling with a tooth and thigh bone to reconstruct for a museum some great, stupid beast extinct with the ice age. Or we are like the louse-bit nomad who finds, in a fold of land between his desert and the mountains, the ruin of parapets and courts, and marvels what kind of

> men had held the world before him. But at least we have the record: the tooth and thigh bone, or the kingly ruins. (3-4)

Though the "facts" are available, the "truth" is elusive.

Neatly and concentrically aligned with these introspective efforts is the reader's attempt to render the action of the novel intelligible. To involve the reader in this way, to force him to reconstruct the work for himself, to finish it, in effect, is the main thrust of *World Enough and Time*—Warren, like Whitman, "expecting the main things" from the reader. In these consecutive interpretive efforts, Warren dramatizes what he has always taken to be the essential human plight: the need "to justify," to reduce one's experience of the world—and of the self—to humanly comprehensible terms. At the same time he implies the continuity of that imaginative activity with the art of reading and interpreting a text.

Beaumont's need to "justify" takes the form of a rigid idealism which is expressed in the stilted and flamboyant rhetoric of the nineteenth-century frontier South. His drama of self-definition often appears to be an unconscious imitation of contemporary melodrama, in which Beaumont imagines himself an ideal Byronic figure capable of transcending the limitations of a corrupt world and triumphantly remaking it as he wills. In these ambitions, Beaumont resembles a host of Warren characters; his fanatical rigidity of mind and his capacity for self-deception, however, are carried nearly to the point of caricature. Not surprisingly, his experience of both self and world proves bafflingly unaccounted for by his idealism; and consequently, his "drama" eventually disintegrates. His is a spectacular and almost ludicrous failure of the moral imagination. Still, the narrator cautions:

> . . . it may have been the drama Jeremiah Beaumont had to prepare in order to live at all, or in order, living, to be human. And it may be that a man cannot live unless he prepares a drama, at least cannot live as a human being against the ruck of the world. (5)

Fiction-making (in some rarefied sense) is exalted here as the quintessential human act. It is self-definition; it is the means by which the human consciousness organizes the "ruck" of experience. Obviously, the world thus discovered is a mirror of self, and the desire for knowledge reveals itself as a craving to know one's self. But "reality" thus invented, Warren seems to insist, is irremediably an artifact: a *fiction* in the less exalted sense of something which is not "true."[6]

This cautionary note of the narrator, therefore, is more significant–and more pessimistic–than it at first appears. The costs of being "human" may, the narrative suggests, include devoting one's life energies to a myth of self and world which are patently false and to a course of action inherently destructive to others as well as to oneself. To take the "worst-case scenario" (the one which the Beaumont plot presents for our contemplation), "living as a human being" may entail an elaborate form of suicide (with complicity in several deaths along the way). In such a world–perhaps characterizable as a "no-win" universe–quintessentially human qualities appear to be primed for failure.

Failure is the dark heart of the novel. The narrator fails, just as Beaumont does, in his interpretative task.[7] For all his nagging inquiry, his evidence-sifting and reflection are ineffectual; the record remains inert and mute to him as well as to Beaumont. The novel's elaborate, multi-tiered structure of fiction-making and interpretation, then, collapses, and the "drama of the unfolding" of significance in the narrative is overwhelmed by the drama of the disintegration of all value and meaning in Beaumont's world.

II

World Enough and Time is dominated by various schemes of dualism which are both historically appropriate to Beaumont's time and place and suggestive of universal moral (or imaginative) dilemmas. Throughout the novel, for all its ironic inversions and convolutions of plot, Beaumont's actions are explained by two simple, contrary terms, flesh and spirit.[8] As described by the narrator, these actions exhibit a similar but not identical polarization: Beaumont is described as moving alternatively outward toward the "world," or inward toward the self, toward objective knowledge or toward solipsism. The major actions of the novel oscillate rather starkly between these poles, with Beaumont frequently colliding with limits and obstacles unaccounted for by his world view. In spite of its complexity, this dialectical movement is so schematically developed one could plot it on a graph. This opposition of separate realms of experience is pervasive, both in Beaumont's account of his life and in the narrator's commentary. Equally important, this interplay of contrasting terms or opposing worlds of experience eventually constitutes a kind of inverted pastoral theme—a topic which will be examined in sections IV and V of this essay.

A solitary and introspective child, Beaumont is badly bitten by his age's version of romantic idealism. His teacher, Dr. Burnham, who writes learned and quaint-sounding treatises on the relation of body and soul, introduces him to the great classical models of heroic behavior, to Christian contempt for the flesh and the world and to Roman fidelity to honor. Through his contemplation of such models, Jeremiah learns to despise the "world" and to revere the "idea"—those transcendent ideas which he thinks capable of redeeming the world.

The same dualism which sunders Beaumont's vision of things is present (according to the narrator) everywhere in his frontier culture, which is posed precariously between civilization and wilderness, spirit and flesh, God and Satan:

> The dirk . . . and the Bible might lie side by side on the table, or Plato and the dueling pistols on the mantel shelf. A man might die for honor or kill for arrogance. In broad daylight the terrible vision of sin might strike [a man] down by the tavern well or back of his own corn crib. It was land of the fiddle and whiskey, sweat and prayer, pride and depravity. (6-7)

A similar dualism is manifested in the political controversy over the issue of replevin, which forms the historical background of Beaumont's tragedy. The Anti-Reliefers (the party of the creditor class) champion a narrowly legalistic concept of justice which has presumably received definition once and for all in the laws of the land. On the other side, the Relief Party (the beleaguered debtor class) appeals to a concept of a justice "higher" than law. In their view, the statutes of men represent only a poor approximation of true justice, and (in relation to their economic distress) the laws of Kentucky seem a mere travesty. While both sides claim the sanction of high principle, both positions are also expedient. Predictably, Beaumont vacillates between the two extremes, but eventually is drawn into the New Court or Reliefer party—approximately the camp whose rhetoric appeals to a higher law.

Early in the novel, the "world" beckons Jeremiah in the form of a handsome inheritance from his maternal grandfather, who embodies almost allegorically the grossness and corruptibility of flesh. Unwilling to pay the price of that worldly success (which involves submitting to the old man's definition of him), Jeremiah seeks the opposite extreme: he will live purely in the spirit, under the tutelage of one Brother McClardy, a backwoods hell-fire and damnation preacher whose text is, appropriately enough, "*Who shall deliver me from the body of this death?*" (30)

In every case, in choosing one pole of his dualistic universe, Jeremiah paradoxically embraces its antithesis; simultaneously, every action in the novel leads him back into himself. Jeremiah's vehement refusal to accept the identity his grandfather would impose upon him is, unconsciously, a gesture of ideal self-definition. Thus, in seeking to gain the world, he discovers himself. Conversely, when Jeremiah finds salvation during one of McClardy's emotion-charged camp meetings, he wanders off into the woods where his ecstatic trance ends in copulation with a repulsive hag. His decision to live in the spirit thus results in the discovery and initiation of his body.

Jeremiah's early flailings in the direction of the "world" (represented by his grandfather Marcher) and the "spirit" (Corinthian McClardy) are eventually followed, however, by what seems an attempt at synthesis–the first of several such efforts. After the death of his mother, Beaumont accepts an offer to read for the bar under Colonel Cassius Fort, a prominent frontier lawyer, planter, and political figure. Fort himself is a mixture of backwoodsman and gentleman, opportunist and man of principle–a man in whom the ubiquitous divisions of self and world are (seemingly) successfully encompassed and contained.[9] He is a man of the world, at ease with it and the apparent master of it. Jeremiah's period of association with Fort represents both a modification of his earlier simplistic dualism and a moderation of his tendency towards abstraction. Under Fort's aegis, Jeremiah appears to move forward toward compromise with the world, toward a sane, if less heroic, accommodation, a life in the community. This characterization of Fort is as much the narrator's as Beaumont's, so it is doubly significant that this potential for compromise or synthesis is never realized in the novel. The reader cannot be surprised that Beaumont's Platonic dualism is treated by the narrator as a misapprehension, part of the historical baggage of the nineteenth century. But when the narrator's terms–*his* dualistic terms—prove no more successful than Beaumont's, the reader is left to grope for more adequate concepts. Fort, playing the role of father-surrogate, suggests a model on which Jeremiah might hypothetically build a successfully integrated identity. But he becomes, in fact, and perhaps even because of his role as father-figure, the man Jeremiah must slay to set himself "free" from the world.

In the same period of his life, Jeremiah has in his friend Wilkie Barron another moral foil who seems, like Fort, to be on enviably easy terms with the world—the taking of pleasure with a thoughtless and natural flair impossible for Beaumont. Wilkie Barron also introduces Beaumont to the plight of Rachel Jordan, a young woman who, Barron reports, has been seduced by Cassius Fort. And it is Wilkie, therefore, who disrupts Beaumont's development toward a pragmatic resolution of the world's and his own divisions and thereby sets the stage for the drama which Beaumont had prepared himself to act. In this first case, the disruption occurs by accident; but in the second and more important instance, Barron acts by design.[10]

Once possessed of Barron's information about his patron, Jeremiah feels himself tainted by association with Fort; his own ambitions seem "poisoned at the root," and he regards Fort as a complete villain (62). Fort had presented to him a certain ideal accommodation with the world, and his crime therefore represents a major disappointment. But the discovery is nonetheless consistent with Jeremiah's presuppositions about the whole fabric of things. Having again found the world corrupt, Beaumont dedicates himself even more single-mindedly to the idea. He resolves to become the champion and protector of the unfortunate Miss Jordan.[11] His discovery of evil in a seeming paragon, then, moves him but one more step on a path he has already chosen.

Warren manages the entanglement of Beaumont and Rachel Jordan as adroitly as he does anything in the novel. Jeremiah's passionless courtship proceeds with the stiff clumsiness of an amateur theatrical. The lives of the lovers imitate the art they both admire: they transform the drabness of their existence into high melodrama. In one stylized tableau, the lovers-to-be meet in the garden, she reluctant and disconcerted, he gravely intense as he recites—appropriately—from Plato's *Symposium*:

> ". . . I read of love, and how a man of high soul may use the beauties of earth as a ladder by which he mounts for the sake of higher beauties, resting

> at last in the single Idea of the absolute Beauty in that life which above all others a man should live to be fully man, the contemplation of the Beauty Absolute." (75-76)

In his homespun facsimile of a romantic ideal of love, Jeremiah finds another solution to the unsatisfactoriness of the world. In the cause of Rachel's injured innocence lies the task worthy of his hand and the motive sufficient to his needs. He will serve Honor as a true knight, releasing Beauty from its bondage.

The most significant "fact" about the courtship is neither its absurdity nor its self-conscious scripting, but the reader's forced recognition that Beaumont is blind to what he is actually about. His account of his behavior is obviously untrustworthy. The best clue to the meaning of his courtship is an earlier scene of Jeremiah as a youth, when he is sexually aroused by contemplating a picture of a female martyr in a book intended for the edification of his soul. Beaumont has been torn between a generous desire to save the woman and an urge to light the fagots at her feet (11-12). His double response to that image best illustrates the irrational, sadistic depths beneath his romantic idealism, and it also presages much of his relationship with Rachel, whom he both serves and victimizes, and whom he treats consistently as an image in a text–an image, in fact, in his text, *his* drama. Thus, the violent pendulations in Beaumont's actions begin to make a kind of sense, at least as symptoms. We know that his motives, the deep sources of the inner life which he records, are completely inaccessible to him. In light of this information, the terms by which he understands and explains his inner drama appear useless as explanation but intriguing as symptoms.

From the first, Beaumont's courtship of Rachel seems to be moving toward a scene of dramatic revelation rather than a consummation. Jeremiah discovers that he must compel her to reveal the "secret" of her seduction and lay upon him the burden of releasing her from its spell. While his aims are initially vague, his pursuit of them is nonetheless ruthless. The psychological pressure he exerts upon Rachel amounts at times to torture (an enacting of his adolescent fantasies about the helpless female martyr). Beaumont justifies himself by appealing to an obscure inner compulsion. "It is because I must," he explains rather lamely (81). In explaining such actions, he continually refers to the authority of his most inward voice, "to the deep truth" inside him. His power to turn all things into impersonal abstractions extends here to his own unconscious impulses, which he exalts as "necessity."

Beaumont eventually triumphs in his strange courtship by compelling Rachel to see the figure of Cassius Fort as the sole barrier between them and happiness. He similarly compels her, without apparent consciousness of it, to charge him with the removal of that specific "obstacle." Even the service of the purest ideal requires, it would seem, a tangible earthly form, and Jeremiah blunders blindly but confidently toward his discovery of that form. Rachel's surrender to his suit is signaled, therefore, not by a declaration of love, but by a command to kill Fort (124)–a command which he has wrenched from her, but which he receives with as much astonishment as recognition. At that moment the shadowy outlines of his destiny come suddenly into brilliant focus: the role he has half-created, half-discovered becomes perfectly clear to him. He is to play the selfless Avenger of Innocence, to kill disinterestedly for the honor of another.

Midway through the novel, then, it emerges that the most significant split or duality in the novel is not between "self" and "world," or "ideal" and base "reality," but in the disparity between Beaumont's conscious intentions and his deeper, unconscious motives. Beaumont's "confession" records his self-conscious grapplings with the meaning of his experience, with the failure of the world to accommodate the structures he imposes on it. But those structures–and the larger "drama" which he prepares for himself–are only superficially explainable in conscious and rational terms. The sources of Beaumont's acts have virtually nothing to do with the stated motives which he offers for them. Similarly, the narrator's attempts to deal with Beaumont's actions and reflections address Beaumont's questions in different terms but on roughly the same level as Beaumont himself–that is, on a rational, intellectual plane. He succeeds in placing the issues in a broader, but not necessarily deeper perspective, at the same time admitting that "explanations can only explain explanations, and the self is gratuitous in the end" (126). The two perspectives thus fail to cohere into something larger (though conceivably they are not intended to) because the commentary (Beaumont's *and* the narrator's) moves on one plane and the action on quite another.

As soon as Beaumont begins his elaborate stalk of his friend and patron, Cassius Fort–and that is the real meaning of the courtship–there is nothing in the commentary adequate to explain what is going on. From that point on, the most obvious thing about Beaumont's behavior is its irrational, compulsive nature. His rationalizations about honor and justice, such as they are, barely disguise the actual drama that is unfolding. That drama takes the form of a familial horror story of betrayal and counter-betrayal involving father and son. Beaumont's obsession consists of a compulsive re-enactment of a pattern of rejection and betrayal of the son (Beaumont) by the father, and the son's subsequent revenge: his rejection and slaughter of the father. Versions of this story are played out–one could almost say rehearsed–several times before the culminating performance with Colonel Fort.

The most obvious instance of this pattern involves Beaumont's rejection of his grandfather Marcher. But strangely, while bitter father/child conflicts are seeded throughout the narrative in the capsule histories of several characters (especially those of Rachel Jordan and Percival Skrogg), Beaumont's own childhood relations with his father appear innocuous. If anything, his own father (Jasper Beaumont), disappointed and embittered by his own failure and relatively meager opportunities, is more conscious of competing with his son than vice versa. As an adult, Jeremiah is outwardly pious and unresentful and remembers his father with respect if not with affection. Like the narrator's need for truth, then, the sources of Beaumont's unconscious needs exist somewhat like a "given" in his character rather than a consequence of anything we can plausibly infer about him. Perhaps the patricidal urge in him is to be understood on a symbolic level only, as a revulsion against the delimiting burden of a specific past, a specific historic identity, and the fact of mortality. Equally plausible–for this is not the only case in the novel–we have an instance of strikingly obvious elements of a theme being presented and reiterated, but failing to form a coherent pattern. So in Beaumont we have a character acting out a *conscious* script which simultaneously conceals as it gives expression to another, *un*conscious drama beneath it–an Oedipal drama of patricide.[12] In relation to this concealed drama, Beaumont's egoism and his desire to play a prominent, noble role on the world's stage become symptoms rather than causes, questions rather than answers. But his unconscious drama appears sourceless and uncaused, or to proceed out of mental processes far below any entity which could name itself "I." Consequently, this unitary character who calls himself Beaumont and is so aggressive about asserting his identity appears, upon close scrutiny, to blur and disintegrate, to become a mask disguising another and quite fathomless agenda.

III

Having taken up his sacred mission to avenge, Jeremiah like Hamlet delays. For more than a hundred pages, the anticipated murder is postponed. During this period, all of the motive forces in the situation change; the whole context is subtly altered–most strikingly perhaps in the scene in which Beaumont receives his second injunction from Rachel to kill Fort (232). On the latter occasion, rather than being compelled by him, she takes the initiative, and her desire for revenge appears genuine and urgent. At this point, it is her will, not his, which is driving the action.

Jeremiah's hesitation after making his great resolve seems, like his previous association with Fort, to point toward a capacity in him for normal, concrete relationships which, under other circumstances, might have developed more happily. A host of small duties as husband and bread-winner, all insignificant in themselves, ensnare him in the world and weaken his "great resolve." Ironically, his developing relationship with Rachel, who is not a creature of unworldly beauty but a woman of flesh and blood, interferes with his pursuit of the ideal she had embodied. During her pregnancy with his child, he discovers himself content with the simple "bounty of common good" (163) in a world he had despised and wished to obliterate. But the greatest irony of this period between Jeremiah's forming his "great resolve" and his actual committing the deed is that he ceases to be his own man, the agent and will behind events and the director-protagonist of his own drama. The self-styled man of action pursuing his great purpose, seeking to perform the "gratuitous act" outside the motives of the world (126), becomes a chip floating on the tide of great events and then an instrument in the hands of a group of conspirators. Beaumont never abandons belief in his "will" to murder Fort or questions the terms by which the act will represent a transcendent solution for him:

> There was Fort. There was the perfect act, outside the world, pure and untarnished. Outside the world, the beginning and the end, the perfect justice self-defining and since defining self, defining all else. (181)

But it nevertheless requires a Machiavellian intervention by Beaumont's political allies to set his "will" in motion. The old scandal concerning Fort and Rachel is resurrected during a bitter election campaign. A handbill apparently signed by Fort in which he denies his former relationship with Rachel and suggests that her child was fathered by a mulatto slave appears mysteriously and is given to Rachel. The shock induces a premature delivery, and Rachel's child is born dead. Only after learning of her miscarriage and its cause–and hearing Rachel's second command to avenge her–does Beaumont act:

> . . . all at once he saw the truth. He had known the world as a trap. He had known that all his life, and he never would have taken its bait had he not taken the sweeter bait of another trap more cunningly concealed. . . . And that trap was the "idea"–the idea itself and pure.
>
> It was perfectly clear. He had lived so long with the idea that that alone had seemed real. The world had seemed nothing. And because the world had seemed nothing, he had lived in the way of the world, feeling safe because he held the idea, pure, complete, abstract, and self-fulfilling. He had thought that he was redeemed by the idea, that sooner or later the idea would redeem his world.
>
> But now he knew: the world must redeem the idea. He knew now that the idea must take on flesh and fact, not to redeem, but to be redeemed. (228)

This tedious intellectualizing, so inappropriate to the situation, nevertheless offers an important insight: even given a killing offense, Beaumont wants clarity more than revenge, his precious self-justifications more than justice. He is obsessed with making sense of his experience, "afflicted with logic as with a disease." Nevertheless, the sense he makes of things appears increasingly paradoxical. Unable to abide ambiguity, he believes that an act must be one thing or another, good or evil, black or white. In that same specious "singleness" of heart with which he has pursued every goal in his life, he goes about testing his idea–the gratuitous blow struck in the sacred name of Justice–by submitting it to the world:

> If the idea could not wear the dark flesh and could not keep its foot firm in the crooked track, what was it worth, after all? I know that that was the last hazard, and like the bold gamester I staked all on a card. I would submit the

> idea to the way of the world. (233)

At the moment of the slaying, Beaumont lifts his mask to reveal himself to his victim. It is an eloquent but empty gesture, and instead of the self-revelation that Beaumont intends, it opens a door into the void. Rather than manifesting his will and vindicating his purpose (thereby defining his identity), Fort's death accomplishes purposes concerning which he is not even aware. Consequently, his simple "definitive act," the quick, decisive blow which leaves the body of his patron and friend Fort lying on his doorstep, is merely another step in the larger dialectic of actions which eventually carry Beaumont beyond the confines of his world view and its meanings.

Beaumont's arrest and trial (the account of which is a small ironic masterpiece), succeed in further undermining his whole structure of assumptions. His own "innocence," partisan of Justice though he feels himself to be, is cast into doubt. Writing in his cell an account of his life, he wrestles with the dilemma of being caught between two separate realms which his action had bafflingly joined:

> "My motive was innocent though my guilt was in deed. Then I rose and paced the room and cried out in my heart against the world in which that happy word can ne'er be single." (327)

Similarly, he finds the privacy of his "secret drama" unsatisfactory. Having killed a man to demonstrate something to the world, he finds his subsequent dissembling odious. He feels himself increasingly torn between the claims of the public world and of his own private stage. "Where did he belong?" he asks himself.

> The problem, however, was more than a problem of doubleness. If the [two] worlds had been entirely different, with a gulf of unplumbed nothingness between, then all might have been easy. He could have lived in both untroubled, speaking different languages, abiding by different laws, worshipping different gods, walking different streets, admiring different landscapes.
>
> But it was not so. The two worlds impinged, overlay and lapped, blurred and absorbed, twisted together and dissolved like mist. That was the trouble. You never knew when the doubleness you embraced might become simplicity, or when the single to which you looked or on which you laid your hand might divide like smoke. . . .(333-34)

The collapse of Jeremiah's discrete categories here presages later and larger shocks. His assurance concerning the nature of the deed he had committed is an early casualty of his experience during the trial. With the collapse, of course, tumbles the framework, the props, the stage settings behind Jeremiah's secret drama of self-definition.

He had believed (like Shakespeare's Brutus) that the blow he had struck was no murder but a sacrifice to a higher good, and that the nature of the act was simply a function of his high intentions in committing it. But the significance of that act proves more elusive. Almost immediately Jeremiah's private motives, and even the act itself, are ironically swallowed up in the larger imperatives of the political struggle. Fort had, on the evening in which he was killed, been about to present a compromise plan to the state legislature on the question of Relief. His untimely murder thus meant the end of possible compromises. The two contending parties turn Jeremiah's trial into a bitter partisan battleground, with Beaumont serving as a convenient bludgeon, this time to be seized and used by both sides, regardless of his guilt or innocence or his high and selfless motives. Beaumont senses for the first time that he is in the grip of powerful forces he can neither fathom nor control and that his fate will not be decided by the quality of the evidence amassed against him or the truth of the charges: "Behind all the words and the waiting, some force was operating that he could not identify" (358).

The case built against Jeremiah is in fact a tissue of lies, half-truths, and honest mistakes: like his own life, it is a fiction, a complete fabrication. Witnesses perjure themselves out of a base hope of gain, or out of partisan feeling, or from sheer maliciousness. But ironically, all the lies "boil down" to the irrevocable "fact" that Jeremiah Beaumont did stab Colonel Cassius Fort, treacherously and in darkness. There is a dark irony in that the half-truths, the unwitting lies which result from the constructions the several witnesses place on poorly remembered events, serve needs of their own and play a part in their own dramas of self-definition, just as the murder of Fort had played in Beaumont's. Jeremiah's own hard certainty concerning what happened dissolves under the impact of these contrary convictions around him (355), and the trial gradually becomes a terrifying paradigm of his life:

> . . . a wandering confusion of talk, half-truth and half-lie, but neither truth nor lie big, a sluggish eddy without drift or direction, with the aimlessness of dream. And, all at once, that was the sinister thing, the eddy, the lack of

> direction, the thought that that was all your life was—a dreamlike confusion that stunk like a rotten backwater when the creek went down. (359)

Like Percy Munn in *Night Rider*, Beaumont feels his sense of identity begin to disintegrate. The "truth" by which he had tried to live, that sustaining illusion of the significance of his acts, crumbles under the pressure of events and cross-purposes. He attempts to re-impose his will on the shape and flow of events by trapping a perjurer with a counter-lie of his own devising, but the effort is discovered and discredits him. Jeremiah's case is destroyed by his own stratagem, and he is sentenced to die.

Thus, neither in the deed itself, nor in the revelation of his guilt, nor even in his contemplation of approaching death, does Jeremiah find that perfect and unchanging clarity of vision or the exaltation he had sought. The climax of his drama eludes him. Instead of arriving at an epiphany, he finds himself losing touch with reality, able to "remember the events [while] the reason that held them together seemed to have fled away . . ." (393). His "definitive act" not only fails to define him in the ultimate sense he desires, but destroys that tentative definition of himself which had brought the act to birth. Furthermore, the crowning irony of this failure is discovered by Jeremiah nine months later: his purely willed act was itself a manipulated scenario, set in motion and controlled by his own friends and political allies. Fort had not sent the handbill which caused Rachel's miscarriage; Wilkie Barron and Percival Skrogg had, knowing that it would trigger a timely assassination useful to their party. Wilkie, his old friend, had directed all. And Skrogg, a pale and intense idealist "wedded to justice" and a man willing to "do anything for that good end," had presumably acted out of motives similar to those which sent Jeremiah to Fort's door in the darkness (323).

After his trial, Beaumont and Rachel act out another strange and stylized romance together. Her declaration of love coincides with the extinction of his last hope of appeal. But in the flesh, Rachel suddenly seems to him rather inadequate to stand as the be-all and end-all of his efforts, the shining ideal for which he had slain a man. "Nothing was as he had planned it" (398). Later, in Jeremiah's underground dungeon, after an appeal to the Governor has failed, they abandon themselves to a passion "as blank and absolute as the face of death that they now confronted" (412). But another passion comes to compete with that one: Jeremiah's need to tell his own story. He confesses to his lawyers; he begins to write an account of his life and an explanation of the reasons for his crime. Like Jack Burden, Jeremiah clings to a belief in his own essential innocence, and again like Burden, he takes refuge in determinism:

> The truth would justify [he thinks], for "if we can truly know the truth we know that it could never have been otherwise, and what we know to be true we can accept, for that is all the heart yearns for in the end." (414)

But having committed himself to truth, Jeremiah finds that knowledge of the truth does not set him free or even release him from his agony. He discovers instead that Wilkie Barron's indignation over Rachel's seduction–a display which had had the consequence of focusing his attention on Rachel–had been feigned: Wilkie had never loved Rachel. Jeremiah's "great resolve" had been set in motion by a lie (416). After learning this "truth," Jeremiah is for a time unable to write. Death becomes for the first time palpably natural to him, and after the horrible nightmare of his own hanging, Jeremiah awakes, feeling

> ". . . nothing now but a numbness and the knowledge without even despair that my life was nothing and all I had ever done was nothing and meant nothing, it was no different from any man's life. Except that I had come to the knowledge." (428)

The "knowledge" he had come to was a shock of disappointment and betrayal–and a sudden intuition of a nihilism undreamt of in his philosophy. Nevertheless, with all ground for hope gone, he continues to write, putting down the words compiling his record–the need to "justify" outliving the hope for personal survival. Completing that record with a final explanatory note, he and Rachel make their ultimate romantic gesture in a way which duplicates his earlier violent gesture of self-definition. They attempt to cheat the hangman with a self-inflicted "Roman" death. This double suicide, while a desperate act, is nevertheless consistent with his previous sense of self and world; it is another Byronic gesture of repudiation. The laudanum they swallow, however, has emetic effects which operate before the poison does its work: "So after the fine speeches and the tragic stance, the grand exit was muffed" (442).

IV

The last section of the book carries Beaumont's career to its conclusion in a Western Swamp, where he is caught—by the terms he has habitually used—in the morass of the "world." At the same time, in the narrator's terms, he is lost in the wilderness which is himself. This last episode moves the action into uncharted territory on several levels. It is entirely Warren's own invention, the original account on which the novel is based having ended with the deaths of the two lovers, J. O. Beauchamp and Miss Ann Cooke.[13]

By freeing himself from the constraints of his sources, Warren manages to disencumber the narrative from its burden of historicity. The narrative moves instead into a murkier nightmare world in which the previously disguised madness and irrationality of the action are exposed. By extending the story into a Western landscape—into the wilderness—Warren also links the Beauchamp/Beaumont tragedy with America's mythology of the West, and with the ambiguous landscape of American pastoral.[14] The protagonist's day-light world takes on the "dream-like confusion" of his nightmares; the landscape not only stinks like a "rotten backwater," it is one.

Implausibly rescued from the hangman at the last moment by the ubiquitous Wilkie Barron, Warren's protagonist seeks refuge in a swampy outlaw domain ruled by the Gran Boz, a hump-backed river pirate whose bestiality is one of the governing metaphors of the last episode. Under his aegis, Beaumont makes his last foray after "perfection" in the terms available under his world view. His service of the ideal having failed him (there being, apparently, no accommodation in this world with spirit), he seeks instead an accommodation "'only in the blank cup of nature, and innocence there'" (506). Still the inveterate dualist, he sinks into animal nature, attempting to extinguish the last vestiges of his humanity in this moral wilderness.[15]

The last section of the novel thus imparts a kind of symmetry to the action—a ruthless symmetry, for one feels that Jeremiah's story has essentially ended long before and that this interminable plot has been drawn out, like a victim on the rack, to reveal every nuance of its "doubleness." The anti-climactic structure of the last section is deliberate: it represents a violation of the conventions of the romantic novel as rude almost as the emetic effect of the laudanum which spoils

Beaumont's grand exit. Moreover, it represents a complete spilling of Jeremiah's experience out of the confines he imagined had encompassed it. His most basic frame of reference is progressively wrenched and disjointed until his experience totally contradicts not only his cherished image of himself but also the terms by which he had defined both self and world. Beaumont's seeking oblivion in the morass of savage "nature" is obviously the antithesis of his former course. Previously, in his pursuit of an ideal beyond the world, he had lived in such a way as to deny his mortal, animal nature. In the swamp, he lives as if he were nothing else. Where he had once sought the "fullness of life above the world," he now seeks a drugged freedom from the pain of consciousness and identity.

The crucible Warren chooses for the metaphysical reduction which Beaumont undergoes is the landscape of the frontier, the storied West—a setting as charged with symbolism as the garden of Rappaccini. Warren does not simply invert the Old World mythology about the New World, redefining the lure of the West in terms radically un-Edenic and un-Paradisical, but like the ancients who located the land of the Dead in a vague, unrealized West, he depicts this landscape as a place of death—both psychic and physical. The promise of the West of a new innocence and new freedom is a mask for its real allurement, which is oblivion. Perfect freedom means the annihilation of self, and that is what Beaumont unwittingly seeks in this "undiscovered country."

The doubleness of the West's seductive appeal is a motif familiar in Warren's earlier fiction, and flight westward is a common part of his usual formula of self-realization. Seeking escape from pain and a new start, Jack Burden "drowns" westward only to come up gasping and unsatisfied in Long Beach. And before *All the King's Men*, in Warren's first novel, *Night Rider* (1939), which is also a chronicle of death-longing, the interpolated tale of minor character Willie Proudfit broadly illustrates the mythic significance of the journey West for Warren.[16] Proudfit goes West and returns successfully—apparently finding himself by losing himself. Proudfit discovers in the West an escape from the burden of selfhood which is so complete as to constitute a kind of surrogate death. But it is a "death" which he survives and which, paradoxically, endows him with the ability to live although scarred by the experience and compelled, like the Ancient

Mariner, to retell his story to strangers.

The same rhythm of flight and return, escape westward to a psychic death and rebirth into a new identity, is present in a more ambiguous form in "The Ballad of Billie Potts" (1943; *Selected Poems, 1923-1975*). There the new identity appears superficial and the return means a fatal confrontation with the father–symbolically, the irremediable, untranscendable past. Again, the promise of escape and transcendence is specious:

> For Time is motion
> For Time is innocence
> For Time is West. (277)

In actuality, the father, the giver of life, awaits the son with the gift of death. This enigmatic poem–one of three haunting works where Warren uses counterpointed voices, a Kentucky landscape, a historical or legendary episode, and a plot of familial betrayal[17]–offers a darker, more sinister version of the writer's cyclical formula of movement towards identity and knowledge. None of the usual cliches about self-discovery or self-actualization seems adequate to account for it, and it ends with the annihilation of the protagonist.

Similarly, Beaumont's flight westward in *World Enough and Time* gives expression to the twin problems of identity and knowledge in a particularly enigmatic fashion. There Rachel sinks into the incipient madness which had threatened her for some time, and they are both mercilessly degraded. Jeremiah willfully abandons himself to the squalor of the place, to drink and gross sensuality. "*Was it all for this, was it all for this!*" Jeremiah eventually asks himself in a moment of horrified realization of what they have become (479). Shortly thereafter, by the most improbable series of events in the novel, Jeremiah and Rachel discover that Wilkie had sent the fatal handbill and precipitated the murder of Fort. Jeremiah, the man of will, discovers that he had been merely a tool, a weapon in the hands of another man.

That information finally frees Beaumont from previously cherished illusions and therefore might appear a positive step. But the same information "frees" Rachel in another sense. In the throes of this revelation, Rachel realizes that Jeremiah had used *her* as an excuse to act out his secret will. She sees that instead of being the agent of his ruin, she has been cruelly used and victimized by him (497-98). In that moment of melodramatic epiphany (significantly, the second occasion that "knowledge" has brought her to attempt suicide), she stabs herself. Thus, Jeremiah is bereft of love and of very nearly the last illusion about what he has done. His life-long secret drama is now stripped of its noble rationalization of selflessness, and his egotism is bared before his own gaze. He sees that he has committed the "unpardonable crime," the crime of self. " 'The crime,' " Jeremiah realizes, "'is I'" (505).

With this insight into his own past behavior, Jeremiah once again attempts to piece together his experience and make sense of it, this time admitting his own errors which he records in a fragmentary journal.[18] He rejects his previous absolutism and the spurious "innocence" he had pretended to, abandoning the quagmire of nature and seeking instead the community of men and an expiation of his guilt. His dream of "innocence," he belatedly realizes, "is what man cannot endure and be man, and now I flee from innocence and toward my guilt . . ." (506). Once again, and for the last time, Jeremiah moves toward synthesis, toward–apparently–a healing of the divisions in his world, though at this point neither he nor the narrator nor the reader can see how that healing might be accomplished:

> "There must be a way whereby the word becomes flesh. There must be a way whereby the flesh becomes word. . . . There must be a way, but I may not have it now. All I can have now is knowledge. But if we can have knowledge, if we can know the terrible logic of life, if we can only know! But at least I know now that life tells no lies in the end, for all the lies, single and particular, will at last speak together in a great chorus of truth in many voices. Thus all the lies and false witness against me told truth, but in my anger and betrayal I did not guess that that is all we need: knowledge." (506)

And knowledge, he announces, "is not redemption, but is almost better than redemption."

As a means of "redeeming" Beaumont from his previous errors or as a resolution of the problems raised by the action, this new "knowledge" appears wholly unsatisfactory. Warren's protagonist persists so long in his errors, learns so slowly and painfully, and (finally) is hurried so precipitously through major psychological changes and epiphanies that his "redemption" does not seem credible. It is all too fast, too schematic. Worse, his state of mind at the end seems a surrender to death rather than an affirmation. Beaumont speaks of a vague expiation of his guilt, but it is the gallows he seeks.[19]

At the end of *All the King's Men,* Jack Burden had found a limited but credible redemption in the fulfillment of the role of husband and citizen and scholar. But Beaumont is more isolated than ever, and though he is described as having forgiven his enemy, there is no credible sign of deep, emotional transformation in him–no Mariner's unpremeditated blessing of the loathesome fellow creatures with whom he shares the earth. If forgiveness is a function of understanding, Beaumont scarcely understands Wilkie enough to forgive him anything.[20] His last determination therefore seems less like the redemptive stirrings of love in his hitherto selfish soul than the taking up of yet a new intellectual position. And whether Warren intended it or not, the total extinction of Beaumont's feelings for Rachel (to say nothing of her "enlightened" suicide) leave the indelible impression that the protagonist has "worked through" love, too, as he has his other illusions. What is left after all his other delusions have been exploded, then, is Beaumont's awareness of the inexorable "logic" of things, which he has observed operating in his own life. A cold comfort by any standards.

Most of all, there seems to be nothing to understand; there is no context to his knowledge. The revelation of Wilkie Barron's complicity in Beaumont's crime obscures rather than clarifies the situation. In the light of this information, Beaumont appears to be a victim himself rather than an egotistical monster who has contrived all in accordance with his secret will. It is, of course, the perfect coincidence of Beaumont's secret will with those forces seeking to manipulate him that begs a larger question, just as the flaws of Oedipus chime with the actions of others to produce both his tragedy and the play's unanswerable questions. In both instances, there is a discernible pattern in events, a "terrible logic" in things, but the pattern doesn't speak a human language. The coincidence of will with external accident–or even with a human malevolence–tells us nothing we can use. With the knowledge of Wilkie Barron's role in events, then, even Beaumont's newly acknowledged "guilt" is undercut. The pattern of naive idealism, arrogance, and pathological obsession which *appeared* to be emerging as an explanation of the action is shattered. The nature of Beaumont's final "knowledge" is therefore impossible to define; his gesture of conciliation is unconvincing and seems more a spasm or reflex than a meaningful act. It seems more plausible to assert that the possibilities of Beaumont's imaginative world have simply been exhausted, completely "played out." His "knowledge" is merely a fatigue deeper than despair.

Nearly all of Warren's fiction has elements of the *Bildungsroman*, and protagonists are typically handled rather roughly and experience profound disillusionment. But Warren ordinarily balances the phase of disillusionment against a phase of recovery and reconciliation. The period of painful loss and knowledge of "separateness" causes flight from reality, but it is followed by acknowledgment of "guilt" and a return, which is a symbolic reintegration of self with world. The latter reintegration is virtually synonymous with Warren's use of the term "knowledge," and all that is involved in the process is perhaps best dramatized in the conclusion of Warren's previous novel, *All the King's Men.* But in *World Enough and Time*, the idea that love might be a form of knowledge–perhaps the redeeming form–is redundantly and savagely parodied in the long drawn-out denouement of the "love" relationship between Jeremiah and Rachel. In the latter, love is merely another trap, another delusion. Beaumont "works through" love as he awaits his execution/suicide attempt and wears out what is left of animal lust in the wilderness, acquiring syphilis instead of insight. Finally, Beaumont's yearning to confess on the scaffold is aborted by his decapitation. In place of a symbolic reconciliation of self and world, Warren leaves the reader with an image of the protagonist's head, that hive of subtlety, with its severed neck encased in the world's clay, being lugged by the assassin back to Frankfort for the reward.[21] The ending thus (to use an ugly but vivid pun) undercuts the very idea of redeeming knowledge.

V

World Enough and Time is obviously Warren's most extreme–that is, his most skeptical–statement of the problem of knowledge, and at the same time, in a bizarre way, it is the most "pastoral" of Warren's early novels, if only in the strict sense of a work in which pastoral conventions are employed extensively. Pastoral images–especially as developed in relation to the New World–form a key part of the symbolic landscape of the last section. Moreover, the pervasive contrast of the two opposing worlds of experience which is the stock-in-trade of pastoral, is the main fact of the novel. The novel participates in the pastoral tradition in somewhat the same way that Marvell's "To His Coy Mistress" (from which Warren derived the title of the book) participates in the tradition of *carpe diem* arguments: it employs the main conventions of the genre but in a way which subverts their usual purposes. In *World Enough and Time,* traditional values associated with pastoral landscape are systematically inverted. In fact, it is hard to imagine a work more bleakly alien to the spirit of pastoral than *World Enough and Time.* Nature is not idealized as simple and uncorrupted; the natural world is Hobbesian rather than Edenic, treacherous as well as harsh, and the unspoiled wilderness of the western frontier is the abode of evil, a sinkhole into which the human disappears. The entire world of frontier Kentucky is a "dark and bloody ground," a breeding place of monsters and moral deformity, with more in common with the mere of *Beowulf* than with the vales or values of Arcady. The past world evoked both by the modern narrator and by Beaumont's "confession" is, in terms of its complexity and general unsatisfactoriness, a mirror image of the present, not an alternative world.

Warren took the epigraph for his novel from the prologue to the fifth book of the *Faerie Queene,* which contrasts (just as Beaumont habitually does) a corrupt present with an ideal "antique world,"

> When good was onely for it selfe desyred,
> And all men sought their owne, and none no more;
> When Justice was not for most meed outhyred,
> But simple Truth did rayne, and was of all admyred.

The relationship of this epigraph to the novel is, of course, bitterly ironic. Warren projects the psychic divisions and uncertainties of the modern age backwards (convincingly for the most part) onto the early nineteenth-century South. Implicitly, there is no such thing as a Golden Age, no lost period of harmony and wholeness; or if there was, the South was far from having any portion in it.

One of Warren's strategies in employing conventions of the genre is to internalize the pastoral landscape within the mind of his protagonist. Pastoral images express not only Beaumont's system of values but his expectations of the world. These expectations, while pervasive, are probably most obvious in the garden scenes where Beaumont courts Rachel by reading Plato's *Symposium* to her, in his reveries of dissolution in wild nature, or in his desires to escape his difficulties in the new land of the West. His deep urge to step outside ordinary life manifests itself during youthful hunts in the Western wilderness. There Jeremiah

> . . . would lie awake and watch the stars and "wickedly" wish he had no family to go back to and that he could stay forever in the forest, "shedding blood and feasting on the wild flesh." All other things to come "seemed of no account and I made only for this life in the great silence and the dark shade of trees." He thought . . . that if a man could stay here he would never grow old and "know the burden of time and things." (16)

In that passage a typically American pastoral image functions as a disguise for unconscious impulses. Beaumont's desire to be exempt from the "burden of time and things," to transcend or escape from reality by sinking into "nature," is obviously a death wish which foreshadows his suicidal urges later in the book. Similarly, after he is convicted of murder and sentenced to death, the strange pleasure he takes in the absolute quiet and darkness of his cave-like underground cell is another expression of this tendency in him.[22]

Pastoral images, then, have little reference in the novel to a real or realizable world; they exist as objects of fantasy rather than as a source of a corrective vision; they disguise things impossible to acknowledge. In Beaumont, the dream of recovered harmony with nature merges into an unconscious death wish. At the same time, his longing for a world partly defined by pastoral imagery illustrates his capacity for self-deception and a general human will to impose self-generated, solipsistic structures upon experience.

Significantly, most of the action of the novel illustrates the failure of the "exterior" world to match up with the "interior" image of it which Beaumont cherishes. The pastoral fantasy and the values they represent are resisted at every point by the world-as-it-is. Experience proves unmalleable to Beaumont's will and, by implication, inherently unaccommodating to human desires.

Pastoral conventions, then, operate in terms of a simple scheme: they represent an impossibly ideal version of an imagined world, rather than an actual past or a golden age of potentiality. The interplay of contrasting modes typical of pastoral is utilized to sharpen the reader's sense of the dichotomy between self and world, to polarize the sentient "I" and the universe outside the self. The pastoral "world" not only lies within, but in Beaumont's psychology, seems reducible to little more than a reality-denying syndrome. The protagonist's interior world, his "idealism," is constantly undercut by the action of the novel and is ultimately dissolved by the corrosive irony of the narrator's point of view, which serves to validate or objectify the harsh actualities of the world in which Beaumont moves. In fact, one of the chief functions of the modern commentator, like the figure of Death in a painting by Poussin, is to deflate and devalue Beaumont's illusions without offering a positive alternative himself. The nature of the "actual" world is therefore largely defined for us by the absence in it of any genuine *locus amoenus*; there is no green retreat which is not delusional. There is neither world enough nor time.

What is at stake in Warren's dark evocation of the pastoral mode may be suggested from one final example from the text. In a letter written from his cell while he awaits execution, Jeremiah Beaumont alludes to a passage from the Roman Lucretius (439) who wrote, appropriately enough for our discussion here, *On the Nature of Things [De Rerum Natura]*:

> For as children tremble and fear everything in the blind darkness, so we in the light sometimes fear what is no more to be feared than the things that children in the dark hold in terror and imagine will come true. This terror, therefore, and darkness of mind must be dispersed, not by the rays of the sun nor the bright shaft of daylight, but by the aspect and law of nature.

Lucretius had articulated here very briefly and succinctly the elemental postulate underlying the rational mindset of Western culture. What Lucretius had asserted and Beaumont wants to assume is the essential order and benignity of nature, which, if known and understood, would dispel the childish "terror" and "darkness of mind" which Jeremiah feels in his own situation. And further, he wants to believe that the nature of things, its "aspect and law," is accessible to–because it is essentially continuous with–his own mind. Beaumont's understanding of the rational hopes of Lucretius is obviously colored by the Romantic epistemology of his own day and by his homespun Platonism. Beaumont's sense of human nature and the larger nature of things form compatible sides of the same coin; man is a microcosm (or metonymy) of greater nature; nature's ultimate order and man's mind are harmonious and mutually intelligible because they form together a larger unity. The pain and terror of life derive, therefore, from ignorance and error and illusion. A solution to–or consolation for–all problems is therefore omnipresent in the discovery of Truth. One need but read nature correctly and interpret its "aspect and law" to return to "Truth" and "natural" harmony–a state long imaged in Western culture in the Myth of Eden and the pastoral idyll. Beaumont is faithful to these precepts till death. It might also be said that Beaumont dies of those precepts and that his disastrous life and decapitation constitute a savage rebuttal of them.

These are ancient and powerful ideas in Western cultures and represent, in various permutations, the *sine qua non* of pastoral tradition–pastoral representing one of the main vehicles for exploration of both our relationship to nature and our distance from an ideal existence. Without an ideal of the harmony or unity of man with nature, pastoral's ubiquitous play of contrasts between simple and complex, natural and artificial, good and evil, is without meaning, and the dichotomous models of life it portrays are incapable of generating either concrete moral judgments or a hierarchy of values. Without that fundamental premise, pastoral cannot organize the worlds of experience which it contains, either morally, intellectually, or aesthetically.

The conclusion of the novel seems to raise these apocalyptic issues; it depicts not just the unpleasant death of the protagonist but the inevitable defeat and destruction of the imagination–at its highest and deepest level of both fiction-making and interpretation. "In the beginning," Beaumont muses near the end of his life, "there was the Word and the Word was with God, but in the end there is the mud and the mud is with me" (481). There is no *Logos*, apparently, and no transcendent order in the cosmos; neither is there a "word," a fragment of text, left in his own life. *World Enough and Time* seems therefore to debunk the possibility of successful integration of self and world and to dismiss the very idea of harmony between man and nature. Finally, the "actual flux of things" in the novel not only appears unstructured and uninterpretable from any point of view available in the work, but inherently unstructurable.

Notes

[1]Bohner's discussion is still one of the most useful introductions to the novel. His use of Warren's essay on Conrad, published a year after *World Enough and Time*, as a commentary on the novel, is particularly suggestive. In his essay, Warren draws attention to the disparity between Conrad's public utterances about his art and the "dark inwardness" of his fiction (42). A similar point could be made about the difference between the reasonable-sounding, persuasive voice which Warren uses in the essay on Conrad and the extreme vision of the novel.

[2]In an interview with Richard B. Sale, Warren has commented that *World Enough and Time* "is based on a counterpoint of style, a counterpoint that has to do with the theme of the book. There is the modern man writing the book, the 'I' of the book. Then there is the Jeremiah narrative which is a period piece, and a period piece in more ways than style. It's a period piece in psychology and other things. It's in a way a set historical piece, the whole thing. But the interplay of the two things offered me the reality, the interest of the novel. . . . The prototype of my character and the me who read the document were the germ of the novel. So me, a modern man, reading that historical document, was the germ of the novel itself" (118).

[3]In an interview with Ruth Fisher, Warren has described the "essence of fiction" as lying in the image it provides of "meaning emerging from experience" (148).

[4]Bohner makes a similar point (93), and James Justus remarks that the "historian's dilemma is ours" (232).

[5]Warren has stated in an interview with Ruth Fisher that the "hero in *World Enough and Time* is a young man trying to create a world for himself, not belonging to this world. He wants to find a cause that will justify a violent and heroic act, as it were. He wants to create a romance for himself to be in. (The book is, in a way, about the pathology of romanticism)" (155).

[6]The passage is remarkably similar in content and language to a point Warren made a year later in his essay on Conrad: ". . . nothing is to be hoped for, even in the most modest way, if men lose the vision of the time of concord, when 'the light breaks on our black sky at last.' That Platonic vision is what makes life possible in its rush and confusion . . ." (54). In the novel, the self-defining drama appears equatable with the "Platonic Vision" of the essay on Conrad.

[7]Barnett Guttenberg, who is willing to entertain the possibility that the ending of the book is darker than his reading of it, also raises the issue of the narrator's reliability (68-69). James Justus, who discusses the narrator's role at some length, comments that the narrator "comes *near* to admitting that even with his help Beaumont's career stretches into trackless territory. . . . we are clearly meant to be wary of placing utter confidence in him" (226; emphasis added).

[8]In the introduction to his edition of Melville's poetry, Warren located the "two poles" of nineteenth-century American thought in Melville's opposition of "nature" and "spirit." Like Warren's protagonist Jeremiah Beaumont, Melville posed the most essential questions to himself in terms of that traditional Western dualism: "What meaning or reconciliation could men find in nature? What in the spirit?" (6). These are precisely the terms in which Beaumont perceives his own experience.

[9]Charles Bohner, on the basis of such figures, finds an essential Aristotelian ethic in the novel: "Man's best efforts must be to try to reconcile these two aspects of his nature" (92). Such a reading overlooks the fact that figures of reconciliation, such as Fort, who *seem* to encompass extremes successfully and to balance self and world, only *appear* to. Begged altogether is the question of how one could reconcile the "black inward abyss" of self with "black outward abyss of nature."

[10]Interestingly, until the culmination of his courtship with Rachel, events appear to be driven by Beaumont's will. Afterwards, external forces increasingly dominate his life.

[11]Beaumont's resemblance to Melville's Pierre is so striking at many points that conscious influence or outright imitation of the nineteenth-century character seems probable.

[12]In a recent essay, Randolph Runyon's examination of some of the patterns of imagery in the novel lends support for seeing an underlying pattern of unconscious Oedipal feeling in Beaumont (71 ff.) Robert Berner's 1960 essay, "The Required Past: *World Enough and Time*," first established the significance of the surrogate father-son relationship between Fort and Beaumont and defined the main import of this motif in Warren's work.

[13]According to Jules Zanger's casebook, the two attempted suicide twice, with the woman succeeding on the second try. Beauchamp died not of his self-inflicted wounds but by the hangman's noose the following day (2).

[14]Beaumont's flight to the Western wilderness fits in several ways the pattern of American pastoral as described by Leo Marx. First, the journey is an "analogue of psychic experience," and second, it follows the three-stage symbolic pattern of self-discovery in its movement from a "corrupt city" to a "raw wilderness" and then back toward the city again (70-71). In my view, that pattern of movement toward self-discovery is not only aborted but parochial in the novel.

[15]Again, Warren's essay on Conrad provides an interesting gloss on the novel: referring to Decoud, Warren comments that skepticism–the "ultimate stage of skepticism . . . has dissolved his identity into nature." His suicide is therefore a repetition of an "already accomplished fate: he has been swallowed up in the immense indifference of things'" (47). Beaumont's plight, then, obviously represents an "ultimate stage of skepticism," and nothing in the conclusion appears capable of refuting it.

[16]This pattern is repeated in almost identical form it the Munn Short episode of *World Enough and Time*, where it has, curiously enough, virtually no impact on Beaumont.

[17]The similarities and other connections among "The Ballad of Billie Potts," *World Enough and Time*, and *Brother to Dragons* are fascinating and deserve study in their own right. *Brother to Dragons*, in fact, appears to be a second attempt to deal with, or perhaps master, virtually, the same "materials" the writer had treated in *World Enough and Time* (but presumably not treated to his own satisfaction). For a treatment of that work, see *Robert Penn Warren's "Brother to Dragons": A Discussion*, ed. James A. Grimshaw, Jr. (Baton Rouge: Louisiana State UP, 1983).

[18]One obstacle to reading this change in Beaumont in a positive way, as an arrival at knowledge of the "Truth," is the curious fact that the text makes a distinction between possession of authentic life and knowledge and the need to write about it: ". . . when you truly begin to live you must construct your own world and therefore have no need for words written on paper, words that can only give a shadow of a world already lived"

(59). The narrator again casts doubt on the efficacy of writing or composing one's life when Beaumont, in prison, claims to have come to "knowledge": "He says [he had come to the knowledge], but we can scarcely believe him, for if he had come truly to the knowledge, would he have sat again the next day at his table and written down the account of . . . [his experience]? With that knowledge what would have been the meaning of that act of recording?" (428). Cited by James Justus (230).

[19]For contrasting views, see Barnett Guttenberg, who views these events as the beginning of the "birth of the true self of the protagonist" (67); and Frederick P. W. McDowell, who claims that Beaumont undergoes "conversion": "He becomes the indisputable tragic protagonist who not only triumphs over the forces that defeated him, but who uses them to attain Grace" (122).

[20]The narrator tells us that all Beaumont "had understood was that Wilkie was at home in the world, was made for the world and the world for him" (453). But later, we are told that Wilkie is another of the book's many suicides, and a particularly inexplicable one (509).

[21]Again, for a contrasting—and more *positive*—view of the protagonist's decapitation, see Marshall Walker, *Robert Penn Warren: A Vision Earned* (Edinburgh: Paul Harris, 1979) 116.

[22]See Randolph Runyon's account of the same tendencies in his essay cited above.

Works Cited

Berner, Robert. "The Required Past: *World Enough and Time.*" *Robert Penn Warren: A Collection of Critical Essays.* Ed. Richard Gray. Englewood Cliffs, NJ: Prentice-Hall, 1980. 67-75.

Bohner, Charles. *Robert Penn Warren.* Rev. ed. Boston: Twayne, 1981.

Fisher, Ruth. "A Conversation with Robert Penn Warren." *Robert Penn Warren Talking: Interviews, 1950-1978.* Ed. Floyd C. Watkins and John T. Hiers. New York: Random, 1980. 138-57.

Guttenberg, Barnett. *Web of Being: The Novels of Robert Penn Warren.* Nashville: Vanderbilt UP, 1975.

Heilman, Robert B. "Tangled Web." *Robert Penn Warren: A Collection of Critical Essays.* Ed. John L. Longley, Jr. New York: New York UP, 1965. 96-109.

Justus, James H. *The Achievement of Robert Penn Warren.* Baton Rouge: Louisiana State UP, 1981.

Marx, Leo. *The Machine in the Garden: Technology and the Pastoral Ideal in America.* New York: Oxford UP, 1967.

McDowell, Frederick P.W. "The Romantic Tragedy of Self in *World Enough and Time.*" *Robert Penn Warren: A Collection of Critical Essays.* Ed. John L. Longley, Jr. New York: New York UP, 1965. 110-24.

Runyon, Randolph. "The Beech, the Hearth, and the Hidden Name in *World Enough and Time.*" *Southern Literary Journal* 17.1 (1984): 68-81.

Sale, Richard B. "An Interview in New Haven with Robert Penn Warren." *Robert Penn Warren Talking: Interviews, 1950-1978.* Ed. Floyd C. Watkins and John T. Hiers. New York: Random, 1980. 101-37.

Warren, Robert Penn. " 'The Great Mirage': Conrad and *Nostromo.*" *Selected Essays.* 1958. New York: Vintage, 1966. 31-58.

—. *Selected Poems, 1923-1975.* New York: Random, 1975. 271-84.

—. *Selected Poems of Herman Melville: A Reader's Edition.* New York: Random, 1970.

—. *World Enough and Time: A Romantic Novel.* New York: Random, 1950.

Zanger, Jules, ed. *A Casebook on the Beauchamp Tragedy.* Philadelphia: Lippincott, 1963.

LOWREY

The Fictive Fetus in *The Cave*

Randolph Runyon

The Cave, James Justus has observed, "is the only one of Warren's novels which lacks a true protagonist" (274). Told from multiple points of view, the novel finds a certain obvious unity in the cave around which its principal characters gather as they participate in or await the outcome of the supposed rescue of the man trapped inside;[1] it finds a subtler and more far-reaching one in the use it makes of some of the elements that recur in the symbolic structure of Warren's five earlier novels.

Though it is true that the novel seems to consist of the various personal histories of Jack Harrick, MacCarland Sumpter, Isaac Sumpter, Jo-Lea and Timothy Bingham, Dorothy Cutlick, and Nick Papadoupalous, and that the story appears at times almost arbitrarily fragmented as it shifts among their different points of view, it is also true that there is one character, and only one, who acts in the present, who is not the mere sum of his past actions, and whose present actions have some effect on the other characters in the novel. Madison Jones has recently suggested that although *The Cave* "has no clear protagonist at all . . . Jack Harrick, the aged and dying blacksmith . . . comes nearest to that role" (51). But the elder Harrick, though both hero and villain of much that occurred before the summer of 1955 when the novel takes place and clearly a character who demands the reader's sympathy, is less the protagonist of the present than its victim. With one exception, the only person who actually does anything of any significance within the time-frame of the novel is Jasper Harrick, but even his having got himself trapped in the cave is a fact in the recent past with which the novel begins and he never appears, as Justus has noted, "except in the flashbacks of the other characters" (275). He is absent from the novel, though he is the absent center around which the plot unfolds. The exception, the best candidate for protagonist because he does act in the present in which the novel transpires, is Isaac Sumpter, who bluffs his way into riches and fame by pretending to relate to Johntown and to the world the hour-by-hour decline of the trapped Jasper Harrick, to whose dying words he has acquired exclusive copyright but which he has in fact invented.

The cave is on land Isaac inherited from his grandmother, and he and Jasper Harrick, an experienced caver, had entered into a partnership to exploit the cave as a tourist attraction. Jasper's interest in caves was in fact an obsession, interpreted by his mother as a desire to escape from his father. "'You made jokes with him,' she said [to Jack Harrick]. 'You'd wink at him. . . . That's why he crawled in the ground. To get away from everything. To get away from the hands on him. To get away from the jokes and the winks. . . . To get away from . . . you'" (298). The hands were those of the Johntowners who had congratulated Jasper as he was about to depart for Korea, telling him he was a chip off the old block, for his father had won a medal in World War I and had emerged victorious in countless backwoods brawls. The paternal winks were given in the hope Jasper would live up to the other half of his father's reputation, that of having seduced half the women in the county. Like Jack Burden in *All the King's Men* —who never could be sure whether Willie Stark had winked at him or not ("'Boss, did you wink at me that time back at Slade's?' 'Boy,' he said, 'if I was to tell you, then you wouldn't have anything to think about.' So I never did know." [16]) —Jasper Harrick was troubled by a paternal wink; what troubled him, however, was not that he could not interpret it but that he did not want to live up to what it meant. Jeremiah Beaumont in *World Enough and Time* provides a closer parallel, since Jasper succeeded in doing what Jeremiah could only fantasize, definitively escape from his father in a cave. What Jasper's mother said about how he took refuge in caves to run away from his father ought to remind us of how Beaumont described the delight he took in crawling into subterranean passages—how he could breathe there

> "the limey, cool, inward smell of earth's bowels . . . a smell cleanly and rich, not dead and foul but pregnant with a secret life, as though you breathed the dark and the dark were about to pulse. And while I lay there, I thought how I might not be able to return, but would lie there forever, and I saw how my father might at that moment be standing in a field full of sun to call my name wildly . . . to no avail." (315)

Yet the similarity between Jeremiah and Jasper ought not to obscure a greater one between Jeremiah and Isaac: Like Beaumont, young Sumpter is trying to make sense of a difficult paternal text, even at the risk of substituting his own interpretation for his father's reading. For what finally pushed the protagonist of *World Enough and Time* over the edge, goading him at last into the madness of murdering Cassius Fort for having seduced the woman who had since become Beaumont's wife, was his receipt of the handbill Percival Skrogg had forged so that it would appear to have been written by Fort, and in which Fort supposedly claimed that the dead fetus to which Rachel Jordan gave birth was fathered not by himself but by one of her slaves. It never occurred to Jeremiah to doubt the authorship of that text, which he took to be a fatherly communication:

> He was grateful to him, not with the old gratitude for favor and kindnesses which had pinched his heart, but with a new gratitude, more profound, like the gratitude of a good son to a father. He was grateful because Fort, with the last outrage, had showed him the truth. (209)

Sons in Warren's other novels are sometimes in a similar situation of seeing themselves the interpreters of a text from the father, sometimes aware and sometimes unaware that the father might not have in fact written it, or that it was not a text in the first place, or that they are misinterpreting it. The wink Willie Stark gave (or did not give) Jack Burden is one such paternal text, though the case for that cannot be made here; likewise, the poem Adam Rosenzweig's father wrote in *Wilderness*, which defined that son's pilgrimage in search of the "worth" that repeated itself in those three lines (5) (and which in the end he found in the *W* [for "worth*less*"] branded on the thigh of a black Moses [217]). The form it takes in *The Cave* is the name Isaac's father gave him, which he persists in interpreting in light of Abraham's willingness to sacrifice his son:

> "[W]hy did you name me Isaac? . . . There wasn't any reason to. There wasn't any Isaac in the family, ever. I have looked at the family Bible." (95)

Reverend MacCarland Sumpter's answer was straightforward enough: "For Sarah conceived, and bare Abraham a son in his old age." But this could not satisfy Isaac, who was certain there was more in that name to interpret, and was especially troubled by the rest of the Biblical paradigm. "'Abraham,'" he countered, "'was so glad that he took the bloody little miracle out in the country and tied him up and was going to cut his bloody little miraculous throat.'" This was not what his father had had in mind at all, but he knew the proper Biblical response:

> "God in his mercy put the ram in the bushes," the old man said, "caught in a thicket by his horns." (96)

Jasper Harrick, caught in the cave on Sumpter's Ridge, might be that sacrificial ram, for at the end of the novel Isaac's father saves his son from the consequences of his son's fiction–from the lies that in fact killed Jasper, preventing real help from reaching him. When MacCarland finally went in himself, he found the corpse still warm–by covering for him, carrying the heating pad Isaac had carelessly tossed aside back to where Jasper lay, collaborating in the concealment of the crime if not in its commission.[2] Yet Isaac persists in his own reading of the text of his name, seeing even this fatherly mercy as the ultimate filicide:

> [I]t was as though there had been a knife, after all.
>
> The old fool had saved him. The old fool had done that and he could never escape that fact. That fact was like a knife blade plunged between your shoulder blades, and you take a step away, and another, and another, waiting to fall. (359)

In this latter-day twist on the Biblical tale, it is not God who tests Abraham but Isaac. "'I was just remembering how the story goes,'" young Sumpter had said to his father when he first asked him about the name, taunting him, almost daring him to live up to his role. "'Wondering how you'd do. Personally, I don't think you'd be up to it'" (96). It is only in retrospect, perhaps, that Isaac Sumpter's role in the botched rescue of Jasper Harrick takes on the appearance of a Biblical Isaac obediently going up the mountain to test his father's ability to save him; at the time, the sequence of events had seemed to Isaac to conform to some other "inner logic" of their own (285).

> It was an accident that Mrs. Harrick had not been for Monty Harrick to go in [the cave where Jasper was trapped]. . . . And it was an accident that . . . Bingham had suggested that he, Isaac Sumpter, should go in. . . . And from

> those words which, upon coming out of the cave, he had heard his own voice, from no intention of his own, saying to the assembled people, all else had followed, step by step, by its own logic. He had planned nothing. (281-82)

It was with a sense of obedience to that logic that Isaac was able to seal Jasper's fate with a clear conscience: "He was nothing, merely the guiltless instrument of a power, but that power, which was not himself, somehow conformed to his will, so that his will was, guiltlessly, achieved and he was filled with the exultation of power" (285).

But that inner logic has another sense as well, for there is yet another drama being re-enacted here. Nearly forty years earlier, Isaac's father and Jasper's had been linked in an awkward alliance that bears an interesting resemblance to their sons' joint exploitation of the cave. Isaac and Jasper, though they may have had more in common than they realized, since each in his own way felt the need for escape—Jasper into caves, Isaac to the greater world beyond Johntown, from which he had returned in disgrace when he was thrown out of college but to which he is desperate to return—would not normally have been friends. Isaac was cultivating Jasper's acquaintance for purely financial reasons; he needed the money for his escape. "He thought how maybe the cave might pay off. But . . . it meant associating with that Jasper Harrick. Suddenly he couldn't bear the thought of Jasper Harrick" (132). Years before, their fathers had for a while been companions in hell-raising but parted company when MacCarland Sumpter got religion and began to preach hell-fire theology to a Baptist congregation. There remained, however, one indissoluble connection between them, Mary Tillyard—whom Jack Harrick first entered and knew in the Biblical sense, but whom in the fullness of time MacCarland came to possess. Jack left to fight the Germans after he knocked Sumpter unconscious for striking him in remonstrance for Jack's too-cavalier account of how he had seduced her; MacCarland took advantage of his absence to marry the girl himself and was later overjoyed, though not without guilt (a guilt it took him forty years to realize), to see that he would not have to be the legal parent of what Jack had fathered on Mary: "[T]hat night when Mary Tillyard had suddenly seized her middle and fallen to the floor, and brought forth the dead child, his heart had leaped with joy. . . . [I]t had been joy, he now knew, in the fact that what would have been the son of Jack

Harrick was dead, was nothing, nothing but a bloody package of offal, and would never stand before him to remind him" (90-91).

Similarly, Jasper Harrick had been the first to find the cave and do the preliminary exploration, while ownership rested with young Sumpter. They would exploit it together, and reap the financial reward, charging admission, developing it into a tourist attraction that would include the nearby and scenic Beecham's Bluff Falls. Jasper's disappearance would have left Isaac the sole proprietor of not only the cave but the venture; Isaac's improvisatory response to that disappearance, however, the "inner logic" he felt constrained to obey, would bring him still greater reward. Isaac had a flair for writing which he displayed when he wrote a newspaper column while still in college, and he knew enough about the media to react quickly to the news of Jasper's entrapment, knew that if it worked in the Floyd Collins case it would work for him. He had a telephone line installed at the mouth of the cave, procured a tape recorder, made a deal with a television station, even opened a bank account in New York where they could send the money. He finagled to get the exclusive right to take food to Jasper as he had schemed for the exclusive right to tell Jasper's story and distracted the authorities by producing an envelope on which Jasper happened to have jotted down the coordinates of his position and instructing them to dig from above, away from the mouth of the cave.

The uterine quality of Warren's caves is at work here and strengthens the analogy between the woman whom the fathers both knew and the cave that brought the sons together. And it does so in imagery specific to the plot of *The Cave*: Mary Tillyard died in childbirth–Isaac's. Specifically, she bled to death. She "ejected from her body the burden that was to be known as Isaac Sumpter, and then nobody could stop the blood" (83). The cave is a virtual fountain of blood, leaving its mark on those who venture in or are otherwise caught up in its imagery: When Jasper's younger brother Monty ran home with the bad news, his mother noticed that the red dust of the cave floor where he had crawled in to look for Jasper had rubbed off from Monty's face onto her own when he kissed her "to give the impression of rouge smeared crazily, drunkenly, on one cheek in wanton dissymmetry" (187-88). This image could have reminded her, as it ought the reader, of another red facial smear, a genuinely bloody one, the one she saw on Jack Harrick's face the first time she saw him, when he returned with the carcass of a bear he had shot: "a smear of blood on the man's face as the man yelled in joy," an image that appears three times in the novel (204 [quoted here], 160, 375). And when Jebb Holloway, whom Isaac tricked into becoming his spokesman in front of the TV cameras and into pretending that he, too, had been in contact with Jasper, leaned against a stalagmite that seemed peculiarly like a beech tree, he began to get the feeling that he was "bleeding to death. It was like blood running out of him from a secret wound . . . and nothing could staunch the wound. He was just bleeding away into the dark beyond the edge of the light made by his carbide lamp" (261).

All this blood has not gone unnoticed. Charles Bohner finds that "Every man is diminished by the death of Jasper, and this ebbing of vitality is symbolized in the novel by the recurring image of bleeding," but complains that "the very profusion of imagery seems a mechanical and calculated intrusion rather than an integral part of the action" (139). If one interprets the bleeding as an ebbing of vitality from the death of Jasper, then perhaps it will seem excessive. But there are other reasons for its pervasiveness, and ultimately they have a great deal to do with the action of the novel.

Nicholas Papadoupalous, in a passage Bohner cites, "felt like he was bleeding away in weakness" (267); what was on his mind, however, was not Jasper Harrick but the fear that some of the people running the food service Isaac encouraged him to set up to feed the crowds that came to gawk at the cave would steal him blind: "He knew he ought to go check receipts, before somebody stole a million dollars off him. . . . It looked like a man could not help things slipping away" (267). Later, when he realized he would not get to make any money after all off the abortion Timothy Bingham was going to arrange for his daughter, he had the same ebbing feeling: "it was like bleeding to death" (326). Jasper Harrick could not have been on the mind of Giselle Fontaine, either, the future Mrs. Papadoupalous, in that scene in an Indianapolis strip joint when the blood on Nicholas's knuckles (who had just bloodied his fist against the jaw of another patron) "reminded her of the blood in her handkerchief, her own blood," the blood she had been coughing more up of lately, since this scene from their courtship occurred long before Jasper got stuck in the cave. Blood was the point where sex and death came together in that instance (her blood and intimations of mortality; Papadoupalous's dream of a resurrected Jean Harlow), a potent compound, for the ecdysiast Fontaine abandoned her art for this ardent admirer, hoping "that his blood might mystically replace whatever blood she had lost, or might lose; that blood-taken-in might, by a mystic homeopathy, cure the disease of blood-going-out" (47).

The promise of such a cure for the hemorrhaging she feared (and would continue to fear [174]) has at least a proleptic function in the novel, for a kind of mystic hemotherapy will take place at the mouth of the cave where Jasper is trapped. Isaac's father will preach to the gathered multitudes (the occasion providing him the same opportunity it does his son to exercise his talent for creative discourse) and many will confess their sins and be saved, singing "Rock of Ages," a hymn that will puzzle Papadoupalous, who "hadn't never got the words straight in his mind except at the beginning. He could not quite make out what the other words meant, about the water and the blood stuff" (266). His interpretative quandary is really our own, for though we might understand the fountain of blood imagery of evangelical Christianity better than he (Papadoupalous was from up north and a Greek), we might with reason suspect that Warren has not simply borrowed that metaphor without giving it a significance and a context of his own. Central to that context specific to *The Cave* (and to the imagery that so consistently appears in his work) is the bloody still-birth (Jack Harrick's illegitimate issue: "a bloody package" [91], "a bloody nothing" [380]) and death in childbirth (Isaac's birth, his mother's death: "nobody could stop the blood") of Mary Tillyard.

These two events are at the origin of a great deal that happens in the novel. The stillbirth of Jack Harrick's son was associated with a fall, which in the passage already quoted appears to have been incidental to an already premature birth: "Mary Tillyard had suddenly seized her middle and fallen to the floor, and brought forth the dead child." But in another account of how it happened, the fall is revealed as the cause itself of the death of the fetus: "Ole Mac Sumpter . . . had married Tillie Tillyard ["Mary Tillyard, whom everybody had called Tillie, but who, to MacCarland Sumpter, had always been Mary" (83): the doubleness of her name will not be without significance] and they were about to have a baby but she had a fall or something and spilled the works right on the floor" (138). In any event, when it happened MacCarland Sumpter's "heart leaped with joy," glad that he would not have to be a father to Jack Harrick's child. In a strangely proleptic analogue to this scene (a scene which transpired years earlier but appears in the narrative twelve pages after its analogue), Timothy Bingham is overcome with joy, too, when he sees his daughter Jo-Lea fall down in the street in front of his bank window: "He knew enough to know that a man had better not mess with joy. A man better have no truck with joy, for there was no telling where it might end" (78). It is an almost inexplicable joy, though at first it seems to come from the superposition of another image upon that of Jo-Lea falling down in the street, Bingham's memory of how she would dry her hair in the sun:

> Jo-Lea Bingham had, for a fact, fallen down, right there on Main Street, in Johntown, and right now was there on hands and knees, her head hanging forward and her hair, jerked loose from ordinary moorings, flung forward over her head. . . . It seemed, preposterously enough, that the girl had chosen that spot of all spots to sun her hair, the way girls do after washing it. . . . (77)

But in retrospect, in light of the joy Brother Sumpter will experience a few pages later when he sees Mary fall and the fetus aborted, and in light of the fact that the abortion Timothy Bingham had been asking Nick Pappy to help him arrange in the pages immediately preceding Jo-Lea's fall was for Jo-Lea herself (and not, as Pappy first thought, for Bingham's employee Dorothy Cutlick), it would seem that that superimposed image is only a cover for the reason for Bingham's happiness. If a fall can abort an unwanted fetus, as it may have done in the case of Tillie Tillyard, then Bingham might well have reason to rejoice, though he gives no sign of realizing it other than his vaguely expressed fear of pursuing the real reason for his satisfaction: "a man had better not mess with joy."

But perhaps the ultimate realization of the reason for Bingham's joy, the fetus behind the scene, should rest with the reader. For if we take seriously his fear that "there was no telling where it might end," taking his hint that it does lead somewhere, if we pursue the echoes of these scenes of falling, we are bound to learn things he could never know. Bingham is not aware, for example, of what Jack Harrick told MacCarland Sumpter about the way he seduced Tillie Tillyard.

According to Harrick, her surrender was premature:

> "I wasn't even prowling for a hand-holt. . . . I wasn't doing nothing worse than counting her verti-bry a little and breathing in her hair, and she of a sudden said, oh, God, and give a moan-like, and it looked like a strut done busted in her. Her knees plain gave down and . . . [s]he would of fallen in the road. If you can call that old grass track a road now." (87)

It was Harrick's insistence that she had fallen of her own accord that made Sumpter hit him, which made him knock Sumpter unconscious, which made Harrick leave town to go to war, which left a pregnant Tillie Tillyard behind for Sumpter to console. And he married her and the child was born dead. So the fall was at the origin of it all, a fall that was so destined to resemble Jo-Lea's fall on Main Street that it had to happen in the road too, a road that was just barely enough a road to be one, "that track up by the old Folsom farm" (86) ("if you can call that old grass track a road").

Neither could Bingham know that when he spread a handkerchief on a rock to sit on outside the cave amid the crowd of spectators to Jasper's plight and then, when he saw his wife Matilda approaching, "quickly retrieved his handkerchief from the rock, as though to destroy evidence" (271), he was re-enacting a gesture Giselle Fontaine had performed when she was to find that there was still more blood on her handkerchief (that, despite marrying the bloody-knuckled Papadoupalous, the homeopathic cure had not taken) and denied the fact in her mind, "crammed the fact down to the bottom of things in her head, like the dirty handkerchief crammed down in the bottom of the laundry basket" (50). A certain handkerchief insisted as well in the scene where Papadoupalous first laid eyes on Giselle Fontaine:

> Time . . . had stopped, because some mysterious element in the scene . . . made an old forgotten fantasy come alive. It came alive out there on the handkerchief-size patch of floor, in the stunning, shattering, noiseless collision of the dimension of Time and non-Time, Dream and non-Dream, which is what we call Truth with a capital *T*. (43)

Something about her reminded him of Jean Harlow. Yet "Giselle Fontaine" was already someone else, and in telling us that, the narrator reminds us that there are some things about a character that even the character does not know:

> standing in a pocket-handkerchief-size patch of open floor . . . the artiste Giselle Fontaine–whose real name was Sarah Pumfret, and who was descended, though she did not know it, from a long line of learned New England divines and talented Pequot-killers. . . . (43)

Two other characters in *The Cave* have two names: Mary/Tillie Tillyard, as noted, and Nick Pappy, "which was what Johntown had decided was a good enough name for Nicholas Papadoupalous" (41). As I have argued in "The Beech, the Hearth, and the Hidden Name," the play on beeches and Beauchamp in *World Enough and Time* suggests what significance can arise from the way the inhabitants of Warren's native region mispronounce proper names. What, then, might underlie Mr. Pappy's, and the fact that these three (Sarah/Giselle, Mary/Tillie, and Papadoupalous) are thus related?

Isaac's insistence on a literalistic reading of his own name may provide a clue. Were he the Isaac he claimed he feared he was, his mother (and he had always been an orphan with regard to her, free to invent the mother he wanted since he had never had a real one: "*He killed my mother,*" he said to himself, alluding to his father, "*so I wouldn't have one*" [332]) would be a Sarah. His father said as much, when Isaac asked him why he gave him that Biblical name: "speaking as though to no one, not even to himself, the man said: 'For Sarah conceived, and bare Abraham a son in his old age'" (96). Isaac never knew that Mrs. Papadoupalous's original name could have fit his fantasy, and perhaps could not have cared if it did; but we could care, knowing how the blood she could not stop coughing up could, without medical intervention, have killed her as surely, though not as quickly, as the hemorrhage that killed Isaac's mother (who "ejected from her body the burden that was to be known as Isaac Sumpter, and then nobody could stop the blood"). "The time came when Giselle Fontaine's fear at what she saw in her handkerchief overcame the fear-prompted denial of the thing seen"–the denial she enacted by cramming the bloody handkerchief out of sight in the bottom of the laundry basket–"and she went to a doctor" (52). But, though treatable, the disease exacted its price; she lost her figure and the color of her hair and became "Sarah Pumfret, who had been Giselle Fontaine" (53).

If she became the Sarah she had always been, with the name of the mother Isaac seems to have always wanted (to become the Isaac his interpretation of his name made him think he ought to be), then it makes sense that her husband's name should undergo a change in Johntown that would make it the equivalent of the local patois for *father*—as the word appears, for example, in the song Jasper's father sings at the end of the novel:

> "I'm coming, son, I'm coming, take your Pappy's hand." (402)[3]

The other woman who had to be spared the sight of a handkerchief, Timothy Bingham's wife, has nothing unusual about her name, except that it echoes—as does Mrs. Pappy's, via the Biblical source—Isaac's mother's. If, that is, the bestowal of two names on a character should sensitize us to the possibility that that character may have a connection to another character that is worth exploring, then the persistence of the first syllable of Isaac's mother's original surname in the nickname by which everyone but his father knew her—the *Till* of *Till*yard, repeated in *Till*ie—should make us wonder if Ma*til*da Bingham might have something in common with the former Tillie Tillyard. Strangely enough, there is a link between them, discoverable through one of those off-hand narrative remarks that are easily forgotten until one suddenly remembers them, that patiently await the discovery of their significance: Timothy Bingham "had got married young, to Miss Matilda Bollin, a sickly, pertinacious, culture-hot and cold-bellied girl several years older than he, who had delivered him first a stillborn son and then a beautiful daughter . . ." (37)—Matilda's first-born, like Tillie's, had been a dead fetus.

In an exchange which would seem to have served no purpose either until now, except to keep alive the notion that the novel is full of local color, Mr. Pappy is confused with Jasper Harrick. It happens because one of the partners in the conversation has been distracted by Jo-Lea's panties (which she left behind, in chapter one, when she got up from a sexual embrace with Monty Harrick to run to the mouth of the cave and call out to Jasper, having suddenly realized he was trapped inside).

> The boy wadded the garment up and stuck it into his hip pocket.
>
> "You might as well keep on admiring and mirating," Jebb Holloway said. "The wrappings is all you got. . . ."
>
> "There is that Greek," Jebb Holloway said.
>
> "I bet it was that Jasper pulled them things off her hen house," the slick-

faced boy said.

"He is shore dark-complected," Jebb Holloway said.

"He ain't dark-complected," the boy said.

"The hell he ain't. He is nigh nigger-complected. Jes you look at him."

"You durn fool, how can I look at him when he is stuck in the ground?"

"Who is stuck in the ground, you durn fool?"

"Jasper Harrick is stuck in the ground, and I bet it was him pulled them things offn' that–"

"Durn," interrupted Jebb Holloway, with high contempt, "if you'd jes git yore mind out of that hen house, you could follow a conversation and a man's line of thinking and know I was talking about that Greek." (222)

Jo-Lea's panties are, indeed, a distraction for a reason other than the one that troubled the slick-faced boy who thought Jebb was talking about Jasper when he was really talking about Pappy. He was concerned with finding out if they *were* hers and if it had been Jasper who pulled them off; and this will, in fact, become a question of considerable importance, fueled by a fiction Isaac Sumpter will invent about Jasper and to which Jo-Lea will contribute a fiction of her own.

But before that happens, this wadded undergarment has a part to play on a stage of the drama of Warren's fiction inaccessible to either Jebb or the boy. This piece of cloth that Jo-Lea "flung aside" (210) in her haste to get to the mouth of the cave, having "stumbled and almost fallen flat" (34) in her haste to extricate herself from them, and which she left by the beech tree, finds a counterpart in the envelope on which Jasper "had scribbled" the compass readings and distances of his path into the cave and which, when he transferred the data into his notebook, under the same beech, he "had wadded up" and "idly tossed" away (134). The panties will remain in their *wadded* state ("The slick-faced boy held something wadded in his hand which he was showing to the other boys" [210]; "He wadded something soft and silky into her hand. . . . 'Yores, they's yores, huh?' " [323]), a persistence that, along with the fact that both the wadded envelope and the panties (both "wrappings," as Jebb Holloway would say) were tossed and flung aside under the same beech tree, makes it legitimate to wonder what it is that connects them in the symbolic underpinning of the novel.

Or, in that of the larger fiction that all of Warren's novels, when read in light of each other, have the power to tell: *Band of Angels*, too, had its "wad of paper, to be flung away" (37) and its "something scribbled on a scrap of paper and flung down in a dark closet" (132). Both of those were texts with paternal connections: the wad of paper to which Seth Parton symbolically reduced Amantha's father and Amantha's soon-to-be-forgotten mental note that her substitute father Hamish Bond walked better than his limp would suggest, respectively.

Now what Jasper idly tossed away later served Isaac in good stead, not to find the way back beyond the fourth chamber where Harrick was trapped but to distract the official searchers away from the fiction he was constructing around the event. In a moment of brilliant improvisation, he faked a call of nature to walk over to the beech to retrieve the envelope he suddenly remembered Jasper had tossed there, and returned to present it to Lieutenant Scrogg (a name that recalls that [Skrogg] of the man in *World Enough and Time* who authored the apocryphal handbill that Jeremiah Beaumont took to be a text from the man who had been a father to him) to persuade him that it would be unnecessary to send surveyors into the cave, that the figures scribbled on the envelope gave Jasper's precise location and that it would be best to dig from above. But–remembering the paternal resonances of equivalent pieces of paper in *Band of Angels* and *World Enough and Time*–what, we have reason to ask, could be paternal about this scrap of scribbled notes Jasper Harrick left behind, and which Isaac–intentionally misinterpreting them–puts to such good use? The misunderstanding that for a moment confuses Jasper with Pappy (in the mind of the slick-faced boy who held Jo-Lea's panties–the equivalent of the scrap of paper Jasper left behind–in his hand) points the way to an answer; the ultimate fiction Isaac is about to invent confirms it.

If MacCarland Sumpter could preach to the crowds gathered at the cave's mouth a gospel of salvation through blood and rebirth, his son is even more persuasive when he issues from within the cave the touching news of a birth to come: " 'Jasper just said, "Tell my girl I love her and would have loved the baby. Tell her I was not going to run out on her. Tell her I was exploring this cave hoping to make a little money for her and the baby" ' " (274). This is great copy. It galvanizes the media and the public, both those assembled at the mouth of the cave and those following the story on television and in print (one newspaper gets the idea to raise money [and thereby its own circulation] for the unborn child). But it is not true: Isaac only pretended to have been in contact with Jasper.

Yet Isaac in his creative journalism had unwittingly stumbled upon something else that *was* true and that had been hidden from the public until now: someone really was going to have a Harrick baby. Moved by the general spirit of confession that his father had been preaching to the same audience ("He said that whoever lives with a guilty secret lives in a dark cave and cannot breathe for the weight of sin. . . . He implored that poor girl [as yet unnamed] to come from the darkness where she lay with the weight of her sin . . ." [320]), and having just been confronted by the slick-faced boy who had found her panties, Jo-Lea Bingham—who was pregnant with *Monty* Harrick's child—stood up and "said she was the one that had lain down in the dark and had in her that baby that Jasper Harrick had put there" (324). When MacCarland Sumpter, having figured out that his son was lying about Jasper's condition and that Jo-Lea's confession had been artificially induced, slipped into the cave to discover the truth and found Jasper dead, his body yet warm (which compounded his son's guilt, for it meant that Jasper could have been saved had Isaac not misled the rescuers), he emerged to announce that Jasper's dying words were that he had impregnated no one, countering his son's lie with one of his own. But the crowd, aided by Isaac's tearful suggestion that his father had not really had the courage to crawl all the way to Jasper, refused to believe this second, more truthful, falsehood.

> "Look at him! . . . Him a preacher and lying!". . . "Yeah, lying—fer that girl—she said it was her!" . . . "Whoop-ee! And she ought to know!" (336-37)

As Lieutenant Scrogg summed it up later, "It is a lot more fun to believe that that Jo-Lea is knocked up. . . . Folks believe what they want to believe" (350). The upshot was that Isaac's fiction was more telling than his father's and more powerful than the truth.

But the power of fiction is such that, in the larger fiction of the novel—in the context, that is, of the complex intertwining of the novel's characters around all its fetuses, double names, misplaced referents[4] and re-enacted gestures—Isaac Sumpter's fiction comes to be a variation on his father's principal story, an unconscious parody of the exhortation to rebirth that was the essence of his preaching at the mouth of the cave. For if the cave which was for the sons what Tillie Tillyard was for the fathers can stand for Isaac's mother and if the man inside it can for an apparently fortuitous but in the end revealing moment be taken for a Pappy, then Isaac's attribution of paternity to Jasper completes his new fictive family circle. By inventing this unborn child he not only succeeds in acquiring enough money and fame to get out of Johntown, but he re-invents himself as well. What gets reborn is Isaac Sumpter, who leaves to begin a new life in New York and a whole new career in a field where his peculiar talents for playing with the truth can be appreciated—"in the world of Big Media" (371).

He has adopted the cave for his mother, has had the unusual opportunity of choosing his own father, and has unwittingly created in the fictive fetus that results from that combination the kind of doppelganger Jack Burden spoke of in *All the King's Men* in his meditation on the "sad little fetus you carry around inside yourself . . . the . . . fetus which is you" (9). Two texts that confront him on his way out of town in the aftermath of what happened at the cave serve as sign posts along his flight that in their combination will remind him, and us, of that fact. The first is, quite literally, a sign:

> He saw a highway sign saying:
>
> SMYRNA, TENNESEE
See the Historic Home of
Sam Davis
Boy Hero of the Confederacy
>
> "Ikey Sumpter," he said aloud, "Boy Hero of the Confederacy." His heart bubbled with gaiety. (367)

The second sign, however, was preceded by a strange, almost unaccountable sense of fear and loathing. In the airport lounge

> his glance fell on an old man, poor, dirty, derelict, with a parcel tied with string, who was sitting over there on a bench. What the hell would such a guy be doing on a plane? That thought—the man's age, his dirt, his poverty, his paper parcel—was a personal affront, a diminution of his triumph, a smear on his pleasure. Then the old man leaned over and picked up from the dirty floor a discarded newspaper. The old man opened the mixed-up sheets, idly, and fixed on something. The sheet held up to the view of Isaac Sumpter was the front page of yesterday evening's *Press-Clarion*. There was the headline:
>
> WOMEN OF STATE RALLY
Mother's Committee Formed to Guard Sweet-
heart and Unborn Child of Trapped Hero
Fund Tops $20,000
>
> (368-69)

If Isaac's automatic reaction to the first sign is to identify with its content, his response to the apparition that preceded the second–the old man with a paper parcel (an apparition akin to the one in *Band of Angels* that troubled Amantha Starr: the hunched-over old beggar she mistook for Rau-Ru [354-55]; and not unrelated, either, to the stranger with a newspaper-wrapped parcel in the short story "Blackberry Winter" whom the narrator "did follow . . . all . . . the years" [87])–is to protest having to be accompanied on his journey to a new life by this objectionable stranger with a paper-wrapped parcel. But Isaac, too, will have to carry some baggage into his bright future. Like Percy Munn's dream in *Night Rider* of a fetus wrapped in newspaper (395), this second sign along Isaac's escape route, the one the old man holds up to his eyes, is a fetus in a newspaper, too, for whose presence in that newspaper Isaac is ultimately responsible.

"Crime," a poem from Warren's *Eleven Poems on the Same Theme* (1942), tells a similar tale. A "mad killer" cannot remember who it was he murdered but carries

> His treasure: for years down streets of contempt and trouble,
> Hugged under his coat, among sharp elbows and rows
> Of eyes hieratic like foetuses in jars;
> Or he nursed it unwitting, like a child asleep with a bauble.

Though Isaac's "heart *bubbled* with gaiety" in response to the first of these signs, the second's uncomfortable message is that, like the objectionable stranger, he will not be traveling alone, that he will have to take along something like this *bauble*, this hugged object that leads to thoughts of fetuses in jars (as did the newspaper-bundled infant in Percy Munn's dream: "a foetus like those which he had seen suspended in liquid in great glass jars" [395]). Those fetal eyes will be upon him even in his "high, spacious office" in New York "with a suffering and *hieratic* canvas of Rouault smoldering on one wall" (370; emphasis added). And he will eventually read the news that Rachel (in *World Enough and Time* the name of the woman who gave birth to a dead child from the shock of seeing a printed handbill whose author arrogated to himself, as Isaac Sumpter did in the case of Jo-Lea, the right to invent the paternity of a fetus to which she had earlier given birth) Goldstein, whose rejection of him had sent him back to the Johntown from which he had gone to all this effort to escape, had–like his mother–died in child bed (372).

Isaac's fictive fetus is perhaps the most striking instance of the way a fetal dream–dating from Percy Munn's nightmare in *Night Rider*, but appearing also in *At Heaven's Gate* when Sweetie Sweetwater meditates on the interchangeability of mummies and fetuses (317), as well as in the passage from *All the King's Men* cited above, and later for example in the Mason jar in which old Miss Pettifew will have buried her illegitimate stillborn child in *Flood* (49)–keeps working itself out in what Warren writes. For here, in *The Cave*, it is the hinge on which the plot itself turns–a plot that is, perhaps, a story about fiction's own creation. At least Warren's.

Notes

[1]Thus, most recently, Madison Jones speaks of "the cave image, which furnishes the center around which the novel turns and to which all the characters, for better or worse, are finally dawn" (52).

[2]Jasper is clearly a sacrificial ram for his own father, who realizes that "*I did not want my son to come out of the ground, because somebody always has to go in the ground. If he was there I would not have to go*" (385). And likewise for Nick Pappy, who "felt a flood of sweet gratefulness" for the thought that "*He is suffering for me. Jasper Harrick, he is in the ground suffering for me*" (270).

[3]The word crops up in conversation as well. Monty Harrick, for example, talking to Jo-Lea about Jasper and his father: "'[H]e had just come out of Pappy's room. I told you how it is. When he goes in to sit with Pappy'" (23).

[4]The slick-faced boy thought Jebb Holloway was referring to Jasper when he was talking about Pappy; when Timothy Bingham asked Nick to make the arrangements for an abortion, he thought that Bingham had got Dorothy Cutlick pregnant, not realizing that he was referring to his daughter Jo-Lea. And it was only when Jo-Lea herself seemed to have become confused about who was the father of her child–when she stood up and announced that she was the unwed mother that she thought Jasper was referring to (but even this was an error induced by Isaac's fiction)–only, that is, through another misplaced referent, that Papadoupalous realized his mistake (324-25).

Works Cited

Bohner, Charles. *Robert Penn Warren.* Rev. ed. Boston: Twayne, 1981.

Jones, Madison. "Robert Penn Warren as Novelist." *A Southern Renascence Man: Views of Robert Penn Warren.* Ed. Walter B. Edgar. Baton Rouge: Louisiana State UP, 1984. 39-57.

Justus, James. *The Achievement of Robert Penn Warren.* Baton Rouge: Louisiana UP, 1981.

Runyon, Randolph. "The Beech, the Hearth, and the Hidden Name in *World Enough and Time.*" *Southern Literary Journal.* 17.1 (1984): 68-81.

Warren, Robert Penn. *All the King's Men.* 1946. New York: Bantam, 1974.

—. *At Heaven's Gate.* New York: Harcourt, 1943.

—. *Band of Angels.* New York: Random, 1955.

—. *The Cave.* New York: Random, 1959.

—. *The Circus in the Attic and Other Stories.* New York: Harcourt, 1947.

—. *Eleven Poems on the Same Theme.* Norfolk, Connecticut: New Directions, 1942.

—. *Flood: A Romance of Our Time.* New York: Random, 1964.

—. *Night Rider.* New York: Random, 1939.

—. *Wilderness: A Tale of the Civil War.* New York: Random, 1961.

—. *World Enough and Time: A Romantic Novel.* 1950. New York: Vintage, 1979.

LOWREY '86

"Secret Sharers" in Warren's Later Fiction

William Bedford Clark

At the end of Melville's *Benito Cereno*, Captain Delano, still something of an American innocent, asks the despondent title character, "what has cast such a shadow upon you?"–and Don Benito answers with two words celebrated for their understatement: "The negro." By now it has become something of a critical commonplace to note that we might pose the same question to any number of Southern writers and receive essentially the same response, for the presence of the black race in America, and, more specifically, the roles that slavery and segregation have played within the framework of our national experiment in democracy have indeed darkened the white South's collective imagination. But unlike Melville's shattered Spaniard, the best Southern writers have resisted the temptation to despair. Instead, they have succeeded in transforming the leaden weight of guilt into a substantial treasure through the alchemy of the literary imagination. Not only has the tragic history of race relations in the South provided the writer with a ready source of dramatic conflict and bitter (though at times decidedly comic) ironies, it has provided him as well with a richly symbolic context for exploring the tensions of the human condition in its entirety. As Robert Penn Warren puts it in his seminal conversation with Ralph Ellison and Eugene Walter, "Race isn't an isolated thing–I mean as it exists in the U.S.–it becomes a total symbolism for every kind of issue. They all flow into it. And out of it" (Longley 40). One of the most pressing issues to emerge from the "race question," the black American's efforts at self-definition within the matrix of New World institutions, in short, his search for a viable identity, has had a particular significance for Warren throughout his career, as we might expect from a writer whose awareness of the fragmentation of the modern Self is especially keen.

This significance is even in the tack the young Warren took in discussing segregation in "The Briar Patch," his much-maligned contribution to the Agrarian symposium *I'll Take My Stand* (1930). Today, that essay is perhaps best read as an implicit gloss on its author's later fiction and poetry, for in it Warren assumes *a priori* that the black man's condition, for all its historical peculiarities, is finally but another version of the human fate. Thus it is that black freedom (in the fullest sense) cannot be conferred upon the race by well-meaning whites, who are themselves saddled with the problematic challenge of selfhood; it must be earned on more than a socio-political level, through the gradual and frequently painful process of individual self-realization. We have here the germ of a later full-blown novel, *Band of Angels* (1955), in which Amantha Starr's ambiguous racial status functions as an informing metaphor for the work's ultimate concern, the shaping of an authentic sense of selfhood through an acceptance of one's responsibility for one's own destiny and an awareness of one's complicity in history, and Warren has explored the symbolism generated by the issue of race in some of his most notable nonfiction as well. In *Segregation* (as its subtitle *The Inner Conflict in the South* suggests), Warren demonstrated that the anguish of the South in the wake of *Brown vs. The Board of Education* resulted not merely from the "division between man and man in society," but from the "many lines of fracture" in the individual Southern psyche, white *or* black (52-53). By the time he published *Who Speaks for the Negro?*, compiled and written during the turbulent period of Civil Rights protests in the early sixties, Warren's revealing predilection for reading racial matters symbolically and his analogous conviction that *all* men and women begin and end with the nagging question of self-integration had fully prepared him to confront Malcolm X, who, as the time's most virulent spokesman for black hatred and rage, represented middle-class white America's greatest fears. "Malcolm X," Warren wrote, "is many things. He is the face not seen in the mirror. He is the threat not spoken. He is the nightmare self. He is the secret sharer" (266).

Such "secret sharers," black characters who function as emblems of guilt or as shadowy *alter egos* for more prominent white characters had already appeared and reappeared in Warren's earlier fiction. We might recall Anselm Jackson in *At Heaven's Gate* (1943), whose determined but ultimately thwarted desire to better himself stands as a subtle rebuke to the personality and career of the novel's principal figure, Jerry Calhoun; or there is the unoffending Phebe in *All the King's Men*, who inadvertently learns of Annabelle Trice's infidelity and whose knowledge results, ironically, in her forced separation from her own husband when she is sold down river into inevitable whoredom. Such characters are, as Leonard Casper noted long ago, "scapegoats," not unlike the slave boy George who is hacked to death in *Brother to Dragons* (1953).[1] But with Rau-Ru (Oliver Cromwell Jones) in *Band of Angels*, explicitly the *k'la* or second self of the tormented Hamish Bond, the black "secret sharer" becomes a considerably more complex character, and the line between victim and victimizer is significantly effaced. Thus, in *Wilderness* we meet Mose Talbutt, who saves the life of the protagonist, Adam Rosenzweig, out of less than altruistic motives and whose confused and crippled humanity undercuts the blind idealism of the naive Adam.

I will not undertake a full accounting of the "secret sharer" as he or she evolves throughout the Warren canon, however worthy that endeavor might be. Rather, I wish to focus here on Warren's three most recent novels, where the "secret sharer" motif persists and where such characters, fully realized as human beings, function not only as foils to the central white protagonists, but to ourselves as well.

At the outset of *Flood* (1964), Brad Tolliver, a failed novelist but successful Hollywood writer back home in Tennessee to work on a movie script about his hometown, has a troubling encounter with a young black man dressed in absurd motley who pumps gas at the Seven Dwarfs Motel. Brad shares with many another Warren character a sense of "savage mirth," a cynical wit that masks his painful vulnerability, and he dubs the young man Jingle Bells and makes a snide remark about his costume. The attendant's dignified response, coupled paradoxically with his obsequiousness–he addresses Brad "respectfully" as "Boss" and "White Folks"–shames Tolliver into giving him a generous tip, at which point the black drops his comic darky accent and persona with an expression that stuns Brad with its unexpected incongruity: "Thanks, Mac." As the shaken Tolliver drives away, Jingle Bells looks up at a billboard image of an "enormous black face" with "bloated minstrel-show lips" and winks (9-11).

We soon learn that Jingle Bells is in reality Mortimer Sparlin, a mulatto with a face like Harry Belafonte, a Lambretta (paralleling Brad's Jaguar), and a degree in Romance Languages from the

University of Chicago. Ostensibly, he has come south for two reasons: to take a seminar in French neo-classical literature from a distinguished scholar at Fisk and to find out what it is like to be a black man in Dixie. But he is also one of Warren's floundering souls, who, like Brad Tolliver, is subject to attacks of nameless fear and lives day-to-day in a private hell of the splintered self. Ironically, Brad's own self-divisions are so intense that at one point he mistakenly envies the black preacher Brother Pinckney (the best-educated man in Fiddlersburg) and even the condemned murderer Pretty-Boy Rountree: ". . . he yearned for the simplicity of purpose, the integrity of life, the purity of heart, even if that purity was the purity of hate, that a nigger must have" (290). The counter-presence of Jingle Bells in the novel testifies to the absurdity of Brad's longing. It is naive enough for Brad to assume that Brother Pinckney and Pretty-Boy, given their respective burdens, live lives that are all of a piece; it is even more self-indulgent for him to assume that the psychic *malaise* from which he suffers is peculiarly his own. Warren takes pains to show that Jingle Bells shares it as well, and with a vengeance.

The final confrontation between Brad and Jingle Bells represents on one level a more fully developed reenactment of an earlier episode in the novel in which Pretty-Boy, presumably out of his inarticulate pain, spits in the face of the white Baptist preacher Brother Potts, who has come to pray with him. Brad has just spent a long-awaited afternoon with Leontine Purtle in the Seven Dwarfs Motel, which has adequately disabused him of the notion that she is a virginal Lady of Shalott, when Jingle Bells provokes him with precisely the kind of cruel and cynical question Brad himself might have posed under different circumstances: "'Tell me, Mac, how do you like blind tail?'" (363). Before Brad can respond with a racial slur, Jingle Bells, a former Golden Gloves champion, knocks him down and proceeds to humiliate him with impunity. The altogether unexpected virulence of Jingle Bells's attack on Brad and the tone of "conniving intimacy" that his taunts assume point unmistakably toward some deeply-seated unconscious identification between the two, and this fact is borne out by Jingle Bells's behavior once the vanquished Brad drives away in defeat. He enters the room Brad and Leontine have just vacated and locks the door behind him. He reclines on the telltale bed:

> Mortimer Sparlin closed his eyes, and knew that the exaltation was gone. He did not know what was left. He pressed his face into the sheet where the odor of flesh and the occupations of flesh faintly lingered. He thought of falling into blackness, for he did not know what was left.
>
> Yes, he did know what was left: the fear. The fear was not of anything in the world. It was of something in himself, and he did not know its name. He did not know what it was, but lying there, he knew that it was in him. He thought: *Something is going to happen.* (365)

What "happens" is that Jingle Bells can no longer stave off the reluctant awareness that he is condemned to be *himself*, nothing more, nothing less. Even with the prospect of a prestigious fellowship in Rome awaiting him, he sees no way out of the prison-house of self. Decked out in the costume of a dwarfish jester, Jingle Bells is more appropriately dressed than the reader has presumed up to now; and Brad Tolliver, though he sports the fashionably nonchalant leisure dress of Southern California, likewise shares his black counterpart's poisoned humor and stunted psyche. Jingle Bells's hatred for Brad is a manifestation of the self-hatred they have in common, a mindless compulsion to strike out against oneself. In the context of *Flood*, Warren makes it clear that such anguish is hardly the exclusive property of a given race. It is the *Angst* the modern consciousness is heir to.

In Warren's ninth novel, *Meet Me in the Green Glen* (1971), the "secret sharer" motif is approached from the distaff side. *Meet Me in the Green Glen* is a brilliant and complex study of the power of love, in its many versions and perversions, as a possible alternative to the alienation and psychic schisms of the contemporary Wasteland. Each of the major characters is a bundle of failures and fears, but finally it is the developing consciousness of Cassie Spottwood that assumes center stage. As a young girl she falls victim to a set of circumstances that deny her the love of Cy Grinder and finds herself trapped in a loveless marriage to Sunderland (the name is suggestive) Spottwood, an older man whose unrestrainable vitality has somehow grown malignant and perverse. Cassie is a woman whose own considerable sexual energy is inexplicably "bottled up"; and when Spottwood is unsuccessful in his attempts to release it, he turns to Arlita, a mulatto woman who bears his child and gradually becomes Cassie's dark second self.

The two women meet for the first time when Arlita, pregnant and uncertain about her future, confronts Cassie with the fact of Sunderland's infidelity. Cassie's first real glimpse of Arlita is significant:

> She had never before seen the Benton woman's face. . . . Now looking at the face, she realized that she had never really seen any Negro's face before. This face was yellow-brown, but the color seemed, in a peculiar way, clear and transparent, as though the air were yellow-brown and what brownness the face seemed to have was the brownness of the air it was seen through. Not that she was, exactly, seeing a white face beyond stained air; she was simply seeing *face-ness*, the fact of a face, some reality she had never guessed. She had the crazy impulse to reach out a finger and touch that face to see if it was real. (89)

For her part Arlita, too, gazes at Cassie with a trancelike intensity, as if she "were musing on the strangeness of something." In the jargon of the existentialists, what we have here is one of those profoundly formative moments in which the Self encounters the Other and thus confronts its own radical Selfness, thus comes to an incipient awareness of the nature of identity. Cassie is the victim of her deadening repression; Arlita suffers from a passionate nature that will not be denied. Both are truncated halves of an ideally whole woman. Ironically, when Sunderland, in conferring forty acres (but no mule) on Arlita as a way of fulfilling his responsibilities toward her, pronounces the two women "neighbors," he is unwittingly articulating the bond that unites the fates of Cassie and Arlita in a bizarre symbiosis.

Years later, however, long after Sunderland has been totally incapacitated by a stroke, the relationship between Cassie and Arlita comes to its grim fruition. Concerned with protecting her daughter from the advances of Angelo, the Sicilian ex-con who in his groping way gradually awakens Cassie to a fuller sense of her own womanhood, Arlita becomes a haunting presence in the white woman's life, seeming on occasion to emerge silently from nowhere, observing Cassie at her most vulnerable moments, not unlike the slaves whose prying glance torments Warren's Thomas Jefferson in *Brother to Dragons.*[2] Arlita is a living reminder of Cassie's inadequacies; and when Cassie, in a strange amalgam of anguish and vicarious fulfillment, eavesdrops on the coupling of Angelo and the girl, Arlita in turn watches her, and then confronts her with the knowledge of her debasement: "'I did'n do nuthen. Nuthen 'cept lay in them cedars and watch you clawen to git in'" (219). Yet, Arlita identifies herself with Cassie as one whom circumstances have rendered old before her time. Like Cassie, she too has been brutalized by Sunderland; and she tells her white counterpart how she once stood with a knife in hand determined to murder him while he slept. Though she blames it on happenstance, Arlita finally lacked the will to carry out her intention at the time; but she nevertheless succeeds in planting in Cassie's susceptible mind the suggestion that eventually leads her to kill her stricken husband with Angelo's switchblade. Cassie's lover is tried and executed for her crime; but in the violent logic of Warren's novel, this injustice ironically makes it possible for both Angelo and Cassie to achieve, however briefly, a level of mutual love that enhances, rather than compromises, selfhood.

To be sure, in the abstract Warren's portrayal of Arlita in *Meet Me in the Green Glen* has its roots in a long tradition in Southern fiction. Indeed, the figure of the vengeful mulatto mistress appears in the novels of writers as diverse in their racial attitudes as George Washington Cable and Thomas Dixon, Jr.[3] Nevertheless, it is impressive testimony to Warren's artistry that Arlita is no mere stereotype or one-dimensional emblem of guilt. A victim, she is fully capable of inordinate cruelty in her own right. Although her life has been obviously circumscribed in many ways by the factor of race, or more particularly, the racial mores of her time and place, Arlita is, in the final analysis, anything but a sociological case history. In her own pained confusion of motives, she is too complex and human to be adequately accounted for through reductive theorizing.

In *Flood* and *Meet Me in the Green Glen*, Warren makes use of his "secret sharer" motif to dramatize the very insight he hit upon, however unconsciously, in "The Briar Patch": All men and women, black *and* white, share in a common bondage; only in facing that fact and the fact of *ourselves* do we begin to loosen the chains that bind us. Only then are communion and freedom possible. In Warren's most recent novel, *A Place to Come To* (1977), he reaffirms this same assumption in precisely the same way. At one point, the novel's narrator-protagonist, Jed Tewksbury, recalls his last talk with his mentor, the renowned philologist Dr. Stahlmann, who, despairing over the degeneration of German high *Kultur* into Hitlerism, will soon take his own life. Renouncing the world that made him what he is, a world he now regards as tainted beyond redemption, Stahlmann has taken the symbolic step of becoming an American Citizen, and thus ostensibly a new man, but, like Brad Tolliver in *Flood*, he also expresses a misguided and ultimately sentimental desire to be black. He explains himself to Jed in this fashion: "'You see,' he said, 'your black man—the black man here—has no history but his blackness. No name but the name stuck on him and not his own. He is the only free man'" (76).

Dr. Stahlmann goes on to assert that the black man is "free" because he "is the perfect existential man," but Jed, even at this stage in his novitiate, can sense the narrowness of his teacher's argument, for he too is hardly a stranger to alienation and estrangement. Nevertheless, Dr. Stahlmann's statement functions as an important reminder that the "existential" quest for authenticity, a theme that unmistakably informs the entire range of Warren's writing,[4] is at the very core of *A Place to Come To*. Significantly, the eventual appearance of a black "secret sharer" in Jed's life helps bring the protagonist's fumbling struggle for individuation into final focus.

After fighting with Italian partisans in World War II and taking his advanced degree, Jed finds himself teaching literature in Nashville, where he once again meets his high school flame, Rozelle. She and her present husband entertain lavishly, and at one of their parties Jed makes the acquaintance of an intriguing character—a Hindu "swami" and poet who has been introduced into the Carrington circle by the sensual and depraved Amy Dabbitt. At a subsequent get-together, Jed is subjected to one of the swami's readings:

> . . . he plunged in, with an effect much like a mélange of R. Tagore, Lawrence Hope, E. B. Browning and Felicia Hemans, not to forget considerable allusion to some handbook of the exotic positions practiced in his native land. Having quickly had enough of such rich fare, I rose as quietly as possible and began to thread my way through female forms seated on cushions, meanwhile murmuring my apologies, and I swear to God that, as my eyes momentarily engaged those of the swami, he almost winked—or maybe did wink—and gave some sort of complex smile that seemed to be full of ironical dimensions involving, among other things, camaraderie, amiable contempt and brotherly knowingness—as though he were just trying to indicate that if I didn't mess with his racket, he wouldn't mess with mine. (253-54)

The swami's conspiratorial wink has its analogues elsewhere in the Warren canon,[5] and Jed's "racket" at the moment consists of carrying on a torrid affair with his hostess Rozelle Carrington. The swami's racket is more ambitious, for, as we learn later, he is at this point in his life a purveyor not only of bad poetry and the wisdom of the East, but of heroin. More importantly, the swami's life as a whole is a bold and elaborate deception that parallels the life of self-evasion Jed seems determined to lead. Years later, when Jed and Rozelle are briefly reunited in Rome, the truth comes out.

The swami is in fact a black man from the South, a graduate of Jackson State who joined the Navy to see the world, jumped ship in India, insinuated himself into the mysteries of Eastern mysticism, and then returned to the United States to work his con. By the time we last hear of him, he is an immensely successful international entrepeneur and the latest husband of Rozelle. Despite Rozelle's insistence that theirs is a perfect relationship, it is clear that the swami is not satisfied with the benefits afforded him by the role he plays so successfully, just as Jed achieves no lasting satisfaction or peace from his role as acclaimed academic, a role he undertakes with the dispassionate and detached rigor of a "good technician." The swami's world has been built around a denial of the past, and it thus serves to deny the self. The same is true of the lives of Rozelle and Jed, and the swami's periodic yearning for soulfood is a comic indication of his desire to derive some residual nourishment from the despised roots he has severed at the cost of his real identity. In *A Place to Come To*, and indeed throughout Warren's fiction, one needs his past and needs to accept it for what it is. Thus, it is only when Jed returns at last to Alabama and is reconciled with the memory of the dead father who has pursued him throughout his life that he can begin to overcome the estrangement that has marked his relationship with others, and himself.

The *alter ego*, whether we call him a *Doppelgänger* or a "secret sharer," is so perennial and pervasive a figure in literature that his appearance in a work of contemporary fiction oftentimes strikes the reader as studied or mechanical, nothing more than the introduction of yet another creaking archetype into the self-reflexive framework of a fictive structure. Generally speaking, such characters seem more at home in a nineteenth-century fabulation like Poe's masterful "William Wilson" than in the more densely realistic novel proper.[6] But I would argue that Warren's persistent use of his "secret sharers" is in no way an instance of conventional literary artifice. In the first place, Jingle Bells, Arlita, and the swami, though developed less fully than the white characters they mirror, are realized as individuals in their own right. We see enough of them to recognize their kinship with us, as well as with their white counterparts in the fiction; and it is only upon reflection that their "archetypal" nature becomes evident. Warren has never been ashamed of the mythic underpinnings of his vision. He has gone so far as to call human history "the big myth we live" (*Brother to Dragons* xiii); but his instinctive suspicion of abstraction, reenforced by the ideas of early influences like Ransom and Tate, has enabled him to bridge the proverbial gap between the particular and the universal. His *mythic* fictions resist the critic's impulse to confine them within a convenient paradigm and at the same time invest the "real" world outside a novel with a renewed sense of the numinous. His handling of the "secret sharers" in his three most recent novels provides us with an admirable case in point.

There is, I would suggest, a more fundamental reason why Warren's "secret sharers" strike us as much more than conventional foils for the author's main protagonists. The persistence with which such characters reappear throughout Warren's writing points toward the intimately *personal* significance the image of the dark *alter ego* holds for him, and we find ready confirmation for such an assumption in Warren's 1975 poem "Old Nigger on One-Mule Cart Encountered Late at Night When Driving Home from Party in the Back Country," in which the figure of an old black junk-dealer returning home to his darkened shack takes on immense significance:

> Brother, Rebuker, my Philosopher past all
> Casuistry, will you be with me when
> I arrive and leave my own cart of junk
> Unfended from the storm of starlight and
> The howl, like wind, of the world's monstrous blessedness,
> To enter, by a bare field, a shack unlit?
> Entering into that darkness to fumble
> My way to a place to lie down, but holding,
> I trust, in my hand, a name–
> Like a shell, a dry flower, a worn stone, a toy–merely
> A hard-won something that may, while Time
> Backward unblooms out of time toward peace, utter
> Its small, sober, and inestimable
> Glow, trophy of truth. (*Selected Poems*, 17)

Here Warren confesses to the presence of his own "secret sharer,"[7] a shadowy brother who suggests the last summing-up in the face of death, when it is no longer possible to flee the naked truth Warren reminds us of again and again—that "we are only ourselves."

Notes

[1]*Robert Penn Warren: The Dark and Bloody Ground* (148). Though Casper's study of Warren's work is now a quarter of a century old, his pioneering insights still warrant attention. Indeed, the Warren critic who dismisses Casper's book as altogether superannuated runs the risk of re-inventing more than one wheel.

[2]In the *New Version* of that "Tale in Verse and Voices," Warren has Jefferson say,

> . . . they spy from the shadow.
> They serve you the dish and stand with face blandly
> Averted, but sidewise that black picklock gaze
> Triggers the tender mechanism
> Of your secret being.
> Oh, they've surprised you
> At meat, at stool, at concupiscence,
> And when you turn inward,
> At the heart's darkest angle you meet
> The sly accusation and the shuttered gleam—
> Sidewise, of course. (69-70; ellipses added)

[3]See Phyllis in Cable's *Gideon's Band* (1914) and Cleo in Dixon's *The Sins of the Father* (1912).

[4]For a thorough, if at times reductive, discussion of Warren's fiction in the light of existentialist thinkers like Martin Heidegger and Martin Buber, see Barnett Guttenberg's *Web of Being*. Though *A Place to Come To* appeared after the publication (in 1975) of Guttenberg's book, his general theses have an obvious relevance to that novel.

[5]One thinks most readily of the scene in which Willie Stark winks at Jack Burden at the beginning of their acquaintance in *All the King's Men* (1946), and of the later, more disturbing scene where Tiny Duffy, who has engineered Willie's assassination, likewise winks at Jack. Note also Jingle Bells's knowing wink at the billboard image of a conventional comic black in that scene from *Flood* discussed earlier in this paper.

[6]To be sure, Warren is something of a fabulator himself, as virtually all his commentators agree. But his narratives are never "fables" pure and simple, for all their "melodrama" and "mythic" elements. The recognizably tangible world we inhabit from day to day is always present, and the best of Warren's critics, like James H. Justus in *The Achievement of Robert Penn Warren*, never lose sight of this fact.

[7]See Victor Strandberg's "Taproots of a Poem: The Long Foreground of 'Old Nigger on One-Mule Cart,'" in Gray (143-154). Strandberg has had much to say about the motif of the other self throughout Warren's poetry in his *A Colder Fire* and *The Poetic Vision of Robert Penn Warren*. As to the "long foreground" of the poem in question, it is worth noting that a prototype of the black man in that work appears briefly in *Flood* (225).

Works Cited

Casper, Leonard. *Robert Penn Warren: The Dark and Bloody Ground*. Seattle: U of Washington P, 1960.

Gray, Richard, ed. *Robert Penn Warren: A Collection of Critical Essays*. Englewood Cliffs, NJ: Prentice Hall, 1980.

Guttenberg, Barnett. *Web of Being: The Novels of Robert Penn Warren*. Nashville: Vanderbilt UP, 1975.

Justus, James H. *The Achievement of Robert Penn Warren*. Baton Rouge: Louisiana State UP, 1981.

Longley, John L., Jr., ed. *Robert Penn Warren: A Collection of Critical Essays*. New York: New York UP, 1965.

Strandberg, Victor. *A Colder Fire: The Poetry of Robert Penn Warren*. Lexington: UP of Kentucky, 1965.

— *The Poetic Vision of Robert Penn Warren*. Lexington: UP of Kentucky, 1977.

Warren, Robert Penn. *Brother to Dragons: A Tale in Verse and Voice–A New Version*. New York: Random, 1979.

—. *Flood: A Romance of Our Time*. New York: Random, 1964.

—. *Meet Me in the Green Glen*. New York: Random, 1971.

—. *A Place to Come To*. New York: Random, 1977.

—. *Segregation: The Inner Conflict in the South*. New York: Random, 1956.

—. *Selected Poems, 1923-1975*. New York: Random, 1976.

—. *Who Speaks for the Negro?* New York: Vintage, 1966.

Toward the Great Amen: Warren's Later Novels

Leonard Casper

Glorying in the seemingly endless flow of Robert Penn Warren's poetry, the steady onset of volumes of fresh and replenished verse, and observing no such effort spent on fiction these past, fast-multiplying years, commentators sometimes lapse into premature final judgments. After more than five decades of winnowing and sifting, critic Calvin Bedient has been perhaps most serenely certain of where the one true literary harvest lies. Dazzled by Warren's virtuosity as a poet, especially since *Audubon* in the late sixties, Bedient finds the fiction hardly tolerable, its "tone a settled drizzle of self-disapproval," the genre itself only "a relative thing, [Warren] wanted the lyrical and the absolute" (17-18): "the novel would never satisfy his tragic passion for inwardness and ultimacy" (17). The later novels particularly are subject to being declared a waste of years whenever, to the wonder felt before the periodic waves of poetry, is added the commonplace conclusion that, of all his fiction, only *All the King's Men* is distinguished enough to deserve to endure. Yet were the prose allowed to be forgotten, how much of the chorus of incries with outcries would be lost? How much of the grand theme of One Flesh, the blood-marriage of earth, water, and sky, so often celebrated in the intense lyrics of Warren but more circumstantially tested in his fully extended fiction would be obscured?

Discussing, in a general fashion, the sources for his *New and Selected Poems: 1923-1985*, Warren has acknowledged the inwardness which Bedient describes: "But some poems do not go into the wastebasket. You, then, take the awful risk of admitting that document as part of yourself. For what is a poem but a hazardous attempt at self-understanding? It is the deepest part of autobiography" (10).[1] The very same historical account, however, reveals similar connections among his life, the life of his times, and the life of his fiction and plays.[2] No one would challenge the fact that Warren's poetry, especially since his remarriage in 1952 and the appearance of *Promises* (1957), has been more open and that, in the process of assuming many personas in each of his novels, there to a larger degree he has withheld his personal self. In a 1970 interview while speaking of similarities, particularly in the feeling for rhythm/pace in both poetry and fiction, he noted to Ruth Fisher only one important difference: "The novels are much more objective for me. The poems have a much deeper and more immediate personal reference" (10).

However, even granting that lyric poetry by definition is interior in its dimensions, so are many portions of Warren's novels. Polarization of the genres becomes even more inappropriate when one considers those aspects of Warren's poetry which are dramatic or narrative, or declarative, or even aphoristic, and are not lyric at all. In these latter examples, which are hardly exceptional, is the problem of voice, of projecting perspective-through-person, intrinsically different from the same problem of Warren as novelist? Is the apparent difference not one of degree only (though the range of degrees may vary greatly from example to example)? Is the writer not trying always to preserve some span of distance between his critical and creative selves, as well as between himself and his reader, and the language that both binds and separates them?

Is there not, indeed, a striking resemblance between the search for self-identity in so many of his poems and the concern of the "objective" novelist who must surrender something of himself to each of his characters, viewed from within, and yet in that same process must hope to gain something of himself from them? Is this dilemma-becoming-paradox not related to the recurring problem that Warren, in poem, fiction, play, has so often vividly portrayed—that of being part of All-Being and yet becoming one's own being, self-fulfilled? Even poems most easily identified as self-centered struggle can be self-transcending. That struggle is as ancient as Adam's wish, through access to superior knowledge, to be companionate with God, having been made in the divine image, and possibly to be one with the Godhead as an equal Person. In the Fisher interview, Warren has said that "the beginning of virtue is . . . to start by making distinctions rather than judgments" (14). But he is too wise to think that valid, persistent distinctions come easily—though judgments unfortunately do. Even the dialectic, a metaphor which he has often used, is too simple in its bipolarization to represent all the tensions and counterforces existent in a single moment. Cass Mastern's web theory (or the tissue of events referred to in his *Selected Essays*) comes closer to our experience of reality refined. Both poetic and novelistic truths as trial assessments press against the membrane of Truth, in anxious hope of some future mystic osmosis. That deep, enduring yearning is the hallmark of Warren's life-work: to be a part of, and yet sufficiently apart from, All That Is. That yearning comes from his vocation as a writer: to be both loner and lover at the same time. Its imprint is on works yet unborn.

If this interpretation is at all sound, it should help restore respect for those novels–*The Cave*, *Wilderness*, *Flood*, *Meet Me in the Green Glen*, and *A Place to Come To*–written during and before the decades when Warren's poetry has unquestionably flourished. Of all the correlatives that might be described or argued, narrative perspective surely is a crucial mode for simultaneously expressing and testing the actualization of the dream of One Flesh. Are alliances implicit even in the most defective or antithetical narrators? What collaborative effects emerge that resemble an achieved collage? Do these seem earned or gratuitously provided?

In some poems such as "Ballad of a Sweet Dream of Peace," Warren speaks directly of the hope to be "all one Flesh, at last" (*Promises* 71); and in "Masts at Dawn" he elevates this hope nearly to the level of prayer: "We must try / To love so well the world that we may believe, in the end, in God" (*New and Selected Poems* 237). He has written a similar number of familial poems, across the years, about his grandparents, parents, and children–only to have to admit that it can be just as difficult, beyond intuition and empathy, to know and understand someone in one's own bloodline as it is to be one with hawk, salmon, cedar, or stone. With the protagonist of "Speleology," therefore, he must sometimes ask "*What is all*?" (*Being Here* 8). Or he may console himself with the thought that "In separateness only does love learn definition" ("Revelation" 304); yet the compulsion remains to acknowledge an infinite intimate interlock ("Oh, nothing is lost" in "Original Sin: A Short Story" 301) even in the absence of some supreme vision to position all animate and inanimate being on some master grid. Without that all-inclusive unity he is not even sure of his own name.[3] To provide compensation, however partial, for this absence he has assembled multiple angles of perspective in suites of poems but more noticeably through contrapuntal arrangements. Numerous critics have commented on the function, for example, of voice variations in "The Return: An Elegy" (311-14), "The Ballad of Billie Potts" (287-300), *Brother to Dragons*, and *Chief Joseph of the Nez Perce.*

In his fiction as well, Warren has tried to be true to the solitariness of his central characters, while still demonstrating that they are not alone in their loneliness and, furthermore, that some of their sense of isolation and even nonbeing is self-imposed and reversible. To show how lives comment on one another, even in the absence of direct communication, he depended on the *exemplum* (what James Justus calls interpolation), a tale within a tale, for *Night Rider*, *At Heaven's Gate*, *All the King's Men*, *World Enough and Time*, and *Band of Angels*. The deployment of auxiliary points of view, however, never quite reached proportions appropriate to a recovered sense of community until *The Cave* (1959).[4] What occurs within young Jasper Harrick, trapped inside a cave, is never once revealed. He remains as mysterious as the minotaur within each of us, awaiting confrontation as the preliminary to self-knowledge. Nevertheless, the very precariousness of Jasper's existence sensitizes many another character to the uncertainty of his own. At first a pattern of sexualism as violation or indifference, in frantic acts of self-assertion, emerges; and the image of the cave as human emptiness is echoed by imagery representing people as wells nearly gone dry and of cancer where "a man's thinking and feeling and living ought to be," and especially of the coffin-like room of Mac Sumpter. It reverberates once again through the many appearances of Jasper's guitar, "The Box," which begins and ends *The Cave.* But the guitar has a special ambiguity, signifying identity's terrible confinement as well as its comforting singularity. Eventually the guitar becomes a communal voice, medium for a folk ballad on the occasion of Jasper's dying, after old Jack Harrick honoring his other son Monty who "has gone in to hold his Big Brother's hand" begins to sing, for himself and all those gathered, "In the dark take your Pappy's hand." That moment is the culmination of a dozen other moments in the novel when, in the absence of words to bring down walls, hands have fallen on hands to provide or ask for solace, in quiet, unconscious communion.[5] No exemplum, no spokesman is necessary for the unvoiced revelation of oneness. It simply accumulates through image and gesture and circulating narration–and through the failure of Ike Sumpter who can give only a dark reading to the saying, "Love is self-betrayal," and therefore is condemned to be "totally himself" only, forever. For the first time Warren's profession of faith derives not from syllogistic convergings in one man's mind nor from the field of force established by the juxtaposing of minor and major characters' tales, but from implications that lap from the confessions of two cornered old men stricken by realization that the loss of their sons greatly matters. The hand on the gut strings is voicebox enough, when the hearts of Jack and Mac give back to life their joyous beat.

Having achieved this bond of moral awareness among men originally hardened individuals, Warren proceeded in *Wilderness* (1961) to test whether the dream of community could be dramatized through a single narrator, thoughtful but not exceedingly introspective, and without reliance on an exemplum to compensate for the narrator's defective intelligence. The result is itself a kind of exemplum with the outer story peeled away; it also resembles a series of poetic images to which, though drastically restricted, circumstantial realism has been restored. Adam Rosenzweig, Bavarian idealist, is born physically deformed, but adds to his sense of alienation by emigrating to enlist in the Union cause during the American Civil War. The months that follow constitute a chronicle of inexperience related by a virtual nonperson, with none of the intellectual pretexts of *The Cave*'s pseudo-Jew, Ike Sumpter. Yet, because Adam's nature is unformed, rather than negative, events impress themselves graphically on him unawares and the narration is sustained impersonally though not subjectively. Without realizing it, his emergent identity becomes a composite of each person he meets: Blaustein, the merchant-prince who adopts him to replace a son killed in battle; Mose, who rescues him during a draft riot; Jedeen Hawksworth the sutler. . . . The process is natural; there is no deliberate seeking of support from others, no acquiescent surrender of selfhood as by Manty in *Band of Angels*, a slave who feels compelled to enslave others to her self-pity. The novel moves quickly from scene to scene with little transition, like a suite of imagistic poems. Adam speculates often about *if's*, but cannot really accept linkages because as an idealist, he resists determinism; yet as a moral coward, he cannot admit the reality of responsibility either. From that poor and incoherent spirit rises the disjunctive nature of this novel, until having actually killed a man on the battlefield, Adam can admit his persistent, secret, innermost motive: a desire to kill a world that is different from himself and from his dream. Adam loses not his innocence but his mask of innocence; yet in his supreme act of hate, at last he understands love—that other men after all *are* men—and is humanized by this admission. In his honesty he proves superior to those self-deceived pharisaic figures described by Warren in *The Legacy of the Civil War: Meditations on the Centennial* (1961), Northerners who claimed to be a Treasury of Virtue, Southerners who played the part of pure victims in a mock tragedy of their own invention, the Great Alibi. Adam's growth in moral awareness implicitly argues for the sameness in all men as prime movers or participants and not merely as passive dupes of circumstance. The core of the concept of human community is properly defined only through acceptance of accountability by all its members.

Attempting to approximate the slow evolution of that solidarity and the mutual obligation of salvation, in *Flood* (1964) Warren returned to a composite vision assembled from multiple narrators. Many are required because especially those who are intellectuals—like writer Brad Tolliver and movie producer Yasha Jones—are so adept at self-deception through rationalization. Yet it is precisely their shared compulsion to communicate and their experience with letting a story "come true" (that is, define itself[6]) in the creative process which finally redeems them. The occasion for their rescue is the imminent death of Fiddlersburg and the reprise of Cal Fiddler's murder of his sister Maggie's alleged rapist. Anticipation of the town's being buried under masses of water gathering behind a government dam forces the characters either to let their memories die along with the town or to review their origins out of concern for the prospective future. Brad manages to come to terms with his literal father once he understands the land to which the man mystically belonged; with his surrogate father, Isaac Goldfarb, whose spirit he learns to revere more than the man's missing bones; and with his editor and third father figure, Telford Lott for whose suicide he admits some responsibility. As for Yasha, he perceives that "You can think of a person as definable only at the point—no, only *as* the point—where an infinite number of lines intersect in flight inward and outward. Person equals point-from-which. And point-toward-which." But he rejects this significant insight by adding cynically, "Which is nothing." Nevertheless, his resistance to involvement diminishes, and he is reborn in Maggie's confession of complicity in her own "rape"; and they are married. Her years of caring for Calvin's mother, while he was in prison, have given her the strength to face herself. Meanwhile, Cal in solitary finally realizes that "there is no *you* except in relation to all that unthinkableness that the world is. And you yourself are." He is purged of his hate at the news of Maggie's pregnancy. Later Brad's ex-wife Lettice finds that her real identity "comes true" as a nurse in New Guinea and lay worker in Chicago, and her letters to him expressing her joy in a destiny she has never fully understood strike a chord in Brad's experience as a writer who has had to learn to let things find and fulfill themselves naturally. He submits to the possibility that "the secret and irrational life of men," all that is inexplicable, may constitute human truth and God's way of writing in crooked lines. Grace may well be mute and therefore misunderstood; but its presence in the gathering design of human lives cannot easily be denied. Original Love preceded Original Sin and still keeps its promises.

A different kind of silence, one of virtual existential shock, permeates *Meet Me in the Green Glen* (1971). Cassie Spottwood has spent almost a third of her forty-odd years tending a stroke-paralyzed husband who never loved her. Young Angelo, recently paroled as a former accessory to robbery, is a fugitive from the vendetta of persons he implicated. Their coming together is inertial, although she tries to believe that he cares for her even when he is unfaithful. Finally, totally frustrated, she kills her husband and fixes the blame on Angelo. Only when the court finds him guilty does she cry out his innocence: and her confession (as with Adam in *Wilderness*) absolves her from her despair, her sense of "lostness and too lateness." Though Angelo is executed anyway and she is institutionalized, a moment of truth has been shared at her outcry in the courtroom and his forgiving answer, "Piccola mia." They have acknowledged each other's essential integrity; each is reborn in the other. Their silence is no longer the sign of living death, but of the limits of language, the open-endedness of life which renders all speech tentative, inarticulate. Other narrators, moved by what they perceive beyond pathos in this couple, confirm the possibility of "coming-closerness"–grace by association, not guilt; love beyond exploitation; the tissue of time which lets all selves, one's own and others', coexist in quiet apposition. Cy Grinder, Cassie's first love, sees in his wife Gladys's face the little girl who is their daughter; and he feels that the person to whom he once turned in his incompleteness is a stranger. That revelation frightens him until he realizes that some day he will be able to try to teach his unborn grandson all he knows and so live on in another. Leroy Lancaster, the trial lawyer, also is moved by the mystery of life to reach out in the dark and take his constantly speechless wife Corinne's hand. All these share the dream of possibility–that the human enterprise, in its wholeness, may not be a waste and a delusion.

Judge Murray Guilfort is part of that enterprise too, but withdraws into an egocentric fantasy world. Envying Spottwood, he pretends that Cassie cares for him and that she never changes, never ages. Both delusions are required by his self-love and inflexibility, the arrest in his own development. He hates the fact that the world is full of people, whom he considers his competitors. Momentarily he understands that love is acquiescence to the mystery of mutual need and that "The dream is a lie, but the dreaming is truth." But that would be to blaspheme against his whole life. Instead, he overdoses on drugs and, dying, sinks into himself, "whatever his self was, as into joy": therefore, into emptiness. Instead of a Vision, the Void.

If *Meet Me in the Green Glen* concerns itself with what silence among the taciturn can manage to convey, *A Place to Come To* (1977) reluctantly concedes the existence of a transcendent cryptic silence beyond the uttermost reach of imaginative speech. Jed Tewksbury, feeling impoverished by the vulgarity of his farmer father, hopes to be heir to limitless far-flung worlds through the study of language. Perhaps the very size of his ambition keeps him constantly a restless, displaced person-in-process. He is never certain whether he is satisfying some obscure destiny or deviating from an identity uniquely his. He is dissatisfied with having made a life out of all that drift and irresolution. Alabama, Siena, Nashville, Chicago, Paris, Florida: wherever he wanders for twenty-five years, he remains to himself a *terra incognita*, the battered image of existential man in frantic search of essence.

The desire to be beyond change—to attain sublime, forever-fixed self-knowledge (to know his name, the poems would say)—forces him with regularity to settle for selfhood too soon: "I was what I was" and "things were the way they were," he declares. What sound like modest advisories, curbing ambition, are actually ploys of a person insisting on a fate that relieves him of anxious responsibility. He confuses identity with "The things that made you what you are and that must be lived by you because you are you"; whereas true *being* involves *becoming* (dynamic change shaped by and shaping certain constants) and *belonging* (mutual assimilation). Jed might have learned his error earlier had he understood his mother's advice: Don't forget who you are, even if you don't know who that is; or if he had cared more about Rozelle Hardcastle, his sometime mistress. Rozelle too, born an orphan and early widowed by murder, then forced into a second marriage of less than love, regularly searches for a stable self-image but settles for surrender to sexual lassitude. These lives inform on one another, but inaudibly. Nor does Jed's too brief marriage to gentle, dependent Agnes—not even her lifted hand on her deathbed—instruct him on the need for human connection, the strength made only from the consummation of weaknesses. His succeeding marriage to Dauphine, once radical student turned abstract idealist, fails as well; and in time, distances even develop between him and his college-age son Ephraim. There is something Jamesian about his failure to perceive that the ever-present "beast in the jungle" is his own insensitivity to others.[7]

Gradually, even literature, the dialogue of many minds insisting on some principle of consonance in an asymmetrical, inchoate world, is not consolation enough. His idol, Dr. Stahlmann, left lonely by the loss of his wife to the Nazis, cannot be saved from suicide by all the books that wall his house. Just as gradually, however, Jed begins to see the interlock of all these lives, as well as those of passing counterparts. More particularly, after his mother's death he finds an affinity with his stepfather, who married the mother he scarcely knew, and learns to hope that some day (like Cy Grinder contemplating his grandson in *Meet Me in the Green Glen*) he will manage to bring his son to all the past places linked with their common lineage. Ephraim will not have to try to be his own ancestor, as Jed once did. Furthermore, committed now to a faith in a timeless, continuous lifeline, he writes to Dauphine asking for the blessedness of her company again. The novel ends on that prayer, rather than on any definite prospect: it is as open as life, to the dream of ripeness or to the nightmare of repudiation.

Warren has moved from his early poetry's call for redefinition, the premonitory warning that all things change, to recognition that there are no finalities *ever* in human experience. (Even individual poems, whether revised or not, have shifted meaning slightly as they have been placed in altered contexts with each new order of selection.) Present tenses never last; therefore, all we most value is essentially indefinable. We live on hypotheses. Yet, we must persist in our pilgrimage toward assumed final meanings and trust that we leave all vanities behind. The alternative is absurdity, acquiescence to nonbeing. But the only being that matters is being with each other and for each other: only then is loving understanding enough, even if loving is itself one of those great indefinables. Nor are inanimate objects left outside this vibrating field of recruiting human force and correspondence. When Jed returns to his birthplace, all the numinous household objects noiselessly summon him from his deep lifelong sleep to his larger self.[8] Similarly, although Jed's life has allegedly been empty, persons, places, and even things are passionately recorded in a community-by-accumulation and convergence (not unlike Adam's experience in *Wilderness*, though many participatory narrators are used in the later novel), all existence incarnated through purpose slowly revealed, more slowly perceived.

So Warren's fiction coalesces with his poetry, both in theme and in substance, creating an organic, dynamic final Flesh. So, too, the New Critic, at his best, views and reviews the intercycling of the nuclear text with all orbiting contexts and distant planes of constellations of every magnitude, as far as the imagination of man can see.

Certainly Warren has never repudiated his own prose. But why the preponderance of poetry late in Warren's life? Perhaps the question answers itself, since surely the later poems anticipate death with the same mixed feelings that any thoughtful person brings to life itself. Is life possible after death? If so, will it resolve all the quandaries and mysteries and quirks of our present experience? Even the surge of curiosity, finally to *know* purpose, must be hedged with other concerns: will all that was never lost now be so glorified by transubstantiality that all love's labor will seem forgotten, and ancestors, wives, children seem wholly other strangers, radiant wisps? [9] If not, what age will they be, once outside of time; how long will unchanging forever seem; will the poignancy of imperfection be missed; how inadequate are our words for such occasions and what will replace them?

Beyond these mingled doubts and affirmations, tested by Warren now in poetic image and anecdote more easily revised toward perfection than the management of long novels might allow, beyond the pressure of foreshortened time irrevocably moving to intersect eternity, there is the opportunity which poetry presents through those personal revelations (though they still conceal many privacies) for Warren to say: Yes, we are just what we are; I know. But what are we? Then, to add finally: You see, I too am anyman and wonder and yearn each day to say Amen: So be it. [10]

Notes

[1]Similar references may be found in Floyd Watkins, *Then and Now*.

[2]James Justus makes numerous biographical references in *The Achievement of Robert Penn Warren*.

[3]In *New and Selected Poems, 1923-1985*, compare such poems as "Sunset" (84), "Ah, Anima!" (153-54), and "Little Black Heart of the Telephone" (160-61). Poems cited are from this edition unless otherwise noted.

[4]The revolving narrative adopted by *At Heaven's Gate* (1943) signified the permanent compartmentalization of its characters, rather than any in-gathering movement toward a common destination.

[5]For a reprise of this gesture in *New and Selected Poems, 1923-1985*, see "Mediterranean Beach, Day After Storm" (256), "After the Dinner Party" (26), "Last Walk of Season" (44), "History During Nocturnal Snowfall" (71), or "Chthonian Revelation: A Myth" (89-90); for the symbol in a different register, hands not quite touching, see the earlier "Mortmain" (263-64).

[6]Warren has said to Ruth Fisher that "the process of writing the novel or the poem, is a process of trying to find out what the writer thinks. He is not working deductively from a highly articulated image, a careful scheme of values; and he is trying to find the values, find the ideas, by a process of trial and error . . ." (4).

[7]See "Vision" in *New and Selected Poems, 1923-1985*: "Can it be that the vision has, long back, already come– / And you just didn't recognize it?" (126-27).

[8]The animation of ordinarily inanimate objects in Warren's poetry parallels the larger measure of such animation in his fiction.

[9]See "Insomnia" in *New and Selected Poems, 1923-1985* (250-53).

[10]In an interview with Thomas Connelly, Warren said: ". . . I'm a yearner; I mean I wish I were religious" (103).

Works Cited

Bedient, Calvin. *In the Heart's Last Kingdom: Robert Penn Warren's Major Poetry.* Cambridge, MA: Harvard UP, 1984.

Connelly, Thomas L. "Of Bookish Men and the Fugitives: A Conversation with Robert Penn Warren." *A Southern Renascence Man: Views of Robert Penn Warren.* Ed. Walter B. Edgar. Baton Rouge: Louisiana State UP, 1984. 95-110.

Fisher, Ruth. "A Conversation with Robert Penn Warren." *Four Quarters,* 21.4 (1972): 3-17.

Justus, James H. *The Achievement of Robert Penn Warren.* Baton Rouge: Louisiana State UP, 1981.

Warren, Robert Penn. *Being Here: Poetry 1977-1980.* New York: Random, 1980.

—. *The Cave.* New York: Random, 1959.

—. *Flood: A Romance of Our Time.* New York: Random, 1964.

—. *The Legacy of the Civil War: Meditations on the Centennial.* New York: Random, 1961.

—. *Meet Me in the Green Glen.* New York: Random, 1971.

—. *New and Selected Poems, 1923-1985.* New York: Random, 1985.

—. *A Place to Come To.* New York: Random, 1977.

—. "Poetry Is a Kind of Unconscious Autobiography." *New York Times Book Review,* 12 May 1985: 10.

—. *Promises: Poems 1954-1956.* New York Random, 1957.

—. *Wilderness: A Tale of the Civil War.* New York: Random, 1961.

Watkins, Floyd C. *Then and Now: The Personal Past in the Poetry of Robert Penn Warren.* Lexington: UP of Kentucky, 1982.

THE POETRY

Poet of Youth: Robert Penn Warren at Eighty

Victor Strandberg

The publication of *Altitudes and Extensions* on Robert Penn Warren's eightieth birthday–April 24, 1985–invites the "Poet of Youth" designation on three grounds.[1] First, as though to prove his contention that a man has all the images he will ever need by age twenty, Warren continues to write extensively about his boyhood throughout the poetry of his septuagenarian years. Second, he continues in this latest volume to explore and develop the themes he first adumbrated fifty to sixty years ago, as though these last poems were designed to fulfill the prophecy implicit in his definition of the image in *All the King's Men*:

> We get very few of the true images in our heads of the kind I am talking about, the kind which become more and more vivid for us as if the passage of the years did not obscure their reality but, year by year, drew off another veil to expose a meaning which we had only dimly surmised at first. Very probably the last veil will not be removed, for there are not enough years, but the brightness of the image increases and our conviction increases that the brightness is meaning, or the legend of meaning, and without the image our lives would be nothing. . . . (126)

And third, when in this fifteenth published volume of his poetry Warren approaches that last veil, the specific image-patterns that dominate *Altitudes and Extensions* obtain their brightness of meaning from an extraordinary impulse toward rejuvenation.

To take up these issues in turn, we may note that the poetry of boyhood comprises about one quarter of the forty-eight poems in this volume, fastening particularly upon intensely vivid first experiences. The awakening to female beauty in "True Love," for example–". . . There is nothing like / Beauty. It stops your heart" (42)[2]–prefigures Warren's theme of epiphanies, whereas the first discovery of loneliness in "Little Girl Wakes Early" (66) calls up a host of poems about alienation. Another salient poem of youth is "Doubleness in Time" (27-

29), where grief slides over to *"Precious Guilt"* (29) as Warren describes the death of mother with an immediacy equal to that of "Revelation" (304-05) and "The Return: An Elegy" (311-14), his earliest and most fervent expressions of filial guilt and sorrow. In "Rumor at Twilight" (18), with his own death a not too distant prospect ("something / Like the enemy fleet below the horizon, in / Its radio blackout, unobserved"), the fireflies glow "like the phosphorescent / Moments of memory" for the insomniac whose head "Dents the dark pillow, eyes wide, ceilingward" while thinking of the lost mother: "Can you really reconstruct your mother's smile?" And doubtless the earliest conceivable memory for a Poet of Youth must be the one (in "The Whole Question" [54]) which takes the mother/child motif back to its infantile beginning: ". . . a strange, sweet taste and bulbed softness while / Two orbs of tender light leaned there above."

But the poems of youth go back even further than this. Though dedicated to Warren's granddaughter, *Altitudes and Extensions* harks back "A hundred and sixty-odd years ago" to his grandfather's prenatal life, focusing upon the spontaneous connections of that fetal condition:

> "a young woman carried it
> In her belly, and smiled. It was
> Not lonely there. It did not see
> Her smile, but knew itself part of the world
> It lived in. Do you remember a place like that?" (49)

Now, in "Re-interment: Recollection of a Grandfather" (49-50), Gabriel Penn (the grandfather) is "lonely / But not alone, locked in my [the poet's] head" (49), where the ancestral "Nails dig at the skull-seam. / . . . stronger and sharper each year":

> I strain to hear him speak, but words come too low
> From that distance inside my skull,
> And there's nothing to do but feel my heart full
> Of what was true more than three-score years ago. (50)

Lost somewhere among those vanished voices and faces is the innermost identity of the octogenarian poet, who is a Poet of Youth most of all because of his unrelenting pursuit of that primal ego which is recoverable only through the medium of the remembered image, or poetry. Most often the recovery of his lost self occurs through an epiphany of the world's beauty, as in "Far West Once" (16-17), where a starlit stream suffices to link the *now* and the *then*: "Able yet, as long ago, / Despite scum of wastage and scab of years, / To touch again the heart, as though at a dawn / Of dew-bright Edenic promise." But the world's beauty, and its evocation of the lost self, can also inflict pain, as when (in "Rumor at Twilight") moonlight recalls the speaker's summons to be an artist in his youth—"A boy who, drunk with the perfume of elder blossoms / And the massiveness of moonrise . . . cried out, / In a rage of joy" (18). Now that boy's hunger "to seize, and squeeze, significance from, / What life is" finds a cynical reply in the adult's poem-ending gesture: "You fling down / The cigarette butt. Set heel on it. It is time to go in."

In "Old Photograph of the Future," the lost self is palpably visible in a seventy-five year old picture of the poet as an infant, but here too the impact of the past is one of reproach to the present self of the observer: "that child, years later, stands there / . . . and he in guilt grieves / Over nameless promises unkept, in undefinable despair" (55). Perhaps the best summary poem of this lapsarian theme is "Covered Bridge," whose title is a metaphor for the dark passage separating the *un*-self—"the boy, sleepless, who lay / In a moonless night of summer, but with star-glow / Gemming the dewy miles, and acres" (47)—from the insomniac adult whose bridge-crossing has meant a loss of identity: ". . . you cannot understand / What pike, highway, or path has led you from land to land, / From year to year, to lie in what strange room, / Where to prove identity you now lift up / Your own hand—scarcely visible in that gloom" (47-48).

Although nothing is more familiar to Warren's reading audience than this theme of lost identity, it becomes re-invigorated in this volume of poems with freshly imagined materials and new intensities of feeling. At the same time, Warren's sixty years as poet have established continuities which impose an overarching coherence linking this last volume to his earliest one, *Thirty-Six Poems* (1935), and its (unpublished) predecessors going back to *Pondy Woods and Other Poems.*[3] The lost anima, in particular—that ideal self of boyhood that found its Edenic home in nature—correlates these latest poems with Warren's earliest ones. In "Mortal Limit" (6) the hawk that rides "updraft in the sunset over Wyoming," its "gold eyes" seeing "New ranges rise to mark a last scrawl of light," traces its genesis in this fashion to a very early poem, "Watershed" (in "Kentucky Mountain Farm"), where "The sunset hawk now rides / The tall light up the climbing deep of air" (317), its "gold eyes" scanning the darkening landscape of the mountains below. Likewise the host of wild creatures moving through time toward their mortal "home" at the end of "The Ballad of Billie Potts" (287-300)—"The bee knows, and the eel's cold ganglia burn / And the sad head lifting to the long return, / Through brumal deeps . . ."—have their parallels early on in *Altitudes and Extensions*: in "Caribou" (8-9), where the animals "move through the world and breathe destiny" (8); in "The First Time" (10-11), where a bull elk stands with "Great head lifted in philosophic / Arrogance against / God's own sky" (11); and in "Minnesota Recollection" (12-14), where an old farmer evinces these creatures' natural dignity when he meets his death by freezing: "His [frozen] face was calm. / It had, you might say, an innocent expression" (14).

As against these anima figures of innocent expression, Warren's lifelong theme of guilt or a fall from innocence also finds strong embodiment in these latest pages. At times the guilt is singular and personal, as in "The Distance Between: Picnic of Old Friends" (41), where a clandestine sexual encounter ends in shame and loneliness, but elsewhere Warren expands the theme of the Fall to a national, historic scale—an enterprise that traces back through *Chief Joseph of the Nez Perce* (1983), the re-written *Brother to Dragons* (1979), and the books about the Civil War. In this new instance, a long poem ironically called "New Dawn" (32-40), national innocence is shattered with the blast over Hiroshima. Written with a journalistic fidelity to fact, "New Dawn" exhibits a peculiarly American psychology of innocence in the crew's willful absorption in the mechanics of their job, with only Tibbets the pilot betraying some signs of misgiving: a "taste like lead" (clearly psychological in origin, not physical) when the bomb explodes; and later, after the awards and the feasting, a sense of alienation ("Some . . . before sleep, consider / One thought: I am alone" [40]).

Among these new poems, Warren's most elaborate treatment of the lapsarian theme must be the first poem in the book, "Three Darknesses" (3-6). Set in "the zoo of Rome," Part I of this poem uses the site where Warren began writing his masterwork on The Fall, *All the King's Men,* in 1939-1940. The poem's central figure, a bear that keeps pounding at an iron door in a cage, recalls the metaphor of an undiscovered self that Warren applied to Willie Stark in that novel: ". . . and the feet would keep on trampling, back and forth like the feet of a heavy animal prowling . . . in a locked-up room, or a cage, hunting for the place to get out. . . . And listening to it, you wouldn't be so sure for a minute the bar or board would hold" (*All the King's Men* 75). The second darkness, in Part II of "Three Darknesses," also evokes The Fall in its snake imagery ("Up Black Snake River, . . . / a snake / . . . / . . . slides off a bough" [3-4]) and in its theme of social isolation: "Nothing human is visible. Each of us lies looking / Seaward. . . . We seem ashamed / Of conversation" (3-4). (This poem also harks back to the poems of the 1930's such as "Monologue at Midnight" and "Picnic Remembered.") And the final darkness, in Part III, is a patient's thought of death while lying in a hospital: "A dress rehearsal, / You tell yourself, for / The real thing. Later" (4).

Within this framework of familiar themes, Warren formulates, in "Three Darknesses," some new answers to the old dilemmas. Most notably, after claiming in Part I that "Since my idiot childhood the world has been / Trying to tell me something," he proceeds past the failure of human communication in Part II to indicate, in Part III, the language in which the world speaks. It is, of course, a language beyond words and names; the world's message must inhere, as in the passage cited earlier from *All the King's Men,* in the image itself. Here at the outset of *Altitudes and Extensions* the image in question is laughably minimal, appearing in a clichéd art form ("an old-fashioned western movie") on a television screen in the sickroom, but it recurs larger and closer throughout this collection as though to profile that "brightness of meaning" mentioned earlier:

> Action fades into distance, but
> You are sure that virtue will triumph. Far beyond
> All the world, the mountains lift. The snow peaks
> Float into moonlight. They float
> In that unnamable altitude of white light. God
> Loves the world. For what it is. (4-5)

By designing his opening poem in this way—having the Three Darknesses end in a small patch of light on a television screen—

Warren anticipates the "old tale told" motif which is the concluding phrase in *Altitudes and Extensions*. It is true that his own "old tale told" in these poems will not be quite like the old-fashioned western, but his poems and the television movie do share one common purpose, which was best defined, I think, by William Faulkner in his Foreword to *The Faulkner Reader*: "To uplift man's heart; the same for all of us: for the ones who are trying to be artists, the ones who are writing simple entertainment, the ones who write to shock, and the ones who are simply escaping themselves. . . . He [the artist] would lift up man's heart . . . because in that way he can say No to death" (x-xi). Warren's most overt instance of saying No to death occurs in his epigraph to *Altitudes and Extensions*, quoted from St. Augustine: "Will ye not now after that life is descended down to you, will not you ascend up to it and live?" But in addition to this epigraph these poems present collectively an imagistic expression of this theme by gradually amplifying the key images in the television picture: light, mountains, the unnamable (or unwordable), God's love.

Always a poet of dialectical impulse, Warren arranges the poems between the beginning and the end of this collection in a loosely contrapuntal pattern. The sunset hawk in "Mortal Limit" (6), for example, which "will accept the mortal limit" much like Wallace Stevens's pigeons at the end of "Sunday Morning," is played off against the airplane in the next poem, "Immortality over the Dakotas" (7), where the passenger rides securely distant from the doomed farmer looking up in the night. The theme of mortality is most intimately treated in Section II, where a pet ("Old Dog Dead"), a parent ("Doubleness in Time"), old friends ("After the Dinner Party"), and the poet himself ("Snowfall") are either dead or prospectively so; but even here a contrapuntal thread of affirmation emerges strongly. "Hope," for example, moves from "the orchidaceous light of evening" to "the promise / Of moonrise" and its "white forgiveness," pausing in the middle to savor the redemption offered by the world's beauty: "While cinders in the west die, the world / Has its last blooming. Let your soul / Be still" (22). And "Why You Climbed Up" portrays the mountains as an agency of quasi-mystical immersion in the world's beauty, from its minimal embodiment ("you will see / The tiny glint of the warbler's eye, see / The beak, half-open, in still heat gasp" [23]) to the panoramic—"on this high ridge, seeing / The sun blaze down on the next and higher horizon." The reward for climbing to this perspective is the mystic's *summum bonum*, cancellation of the ego, "As though to forget and leave / All things, great and small, you call / The past, all things, great and small, you call / The Self"; but, of course, the lapse back to individual identity recurs with the descent from the mountain–". . . stumbling, down. / Then all begins again. And you are you." Concluding Section II, "Snowfall" moves toward a remarkably serene reconciliation with mortality. The poem first gathers a lifetime of good memories like the harvest suggested by Lear's "Ripeness is all" ("What year will you know the fruit that is yourself?" [30]), and then portrays the snow coming over this landscape of memory as a final fulfillment–"and you / Stand in the darkness of whiteness / Which is the perfection of Being" (31).

The capital letter in "perfection of Being" relates this poem to the motif of God's love back in "Three Darknesses." (Earlier poems like "A Way to Love God" in the *Arcturus* collection and "Interjection #6" in *Or Else* also sanctified death in this way.) To say No to death by seeing it as "the perfection of Being" may raise suspicions of sophistry, but analogues spring to mind from impeccable sources–Whitman's accolade to death in Section 49 of *Song of Myself*, for example: "O grass of graves–O perpetual transfers and promotions." Warren's own pantheistic sensibility traces back to his earliest work as a poet. In Poem II of "Kentucky Mountain Farm"–a poem of the 1920's–a pantheistic deity receives its own worn-out phenomena returning down the stream of time:

> . . . the fractured atoms now are borne
> Down shifting waters to the tall, profound
> Shadow of the absolute deeps,
> Wherein the spirit moves and never sleeps
> That held the foot among the rocks, that bound
> The tired hand upon the stubborn plow,
> Knotted the flesh unto the hungry bone,
> The redbud to the charred and broken bough,
> And strung the bitter tendons of the stone. (316)

The primary difference between this early poetry and that of the 1980's is of tone rather than concept. Words like "fractured," "tired," "hungry," "broken," and "bitter," indicative of the influence of *The Waste Land* in the 1920's, give way to a tone of acceptance and celebration in the late volumes. Here in *Altitudes and Extensions*,

"Last Walk of Season" (44) presents a notable instance of that celebratory spirit. Placed near the middle of this collection, it evokes the crucial motifs from the television scene–light, mountains, the unnamable love of the world for what it is–but they now assume an imminent magnitude as opposed to the small-screen image of their original appearance. As its title implies, "Last Walk of Season" is a poem of farewell, perhaps permanent, to the world's beauty: "For the last time . . . we climb / In the westward hour, up the mountain trail / To see the last light." In that last light, with "No cloud in the washed evening," a Wordsworthian immersion in nature gradually ensues as the eye again moves from the minimal ("How bright, / Rain-washed, the pebbles shine!") to an overview of a mountain lake: "Beyond it, the sun, / Ghostly, dips, flame-huddled in mist. We undertake / Not to exist, except as part of that one / Existence." At this level of intensity, the theme of the unnamable comes into play, bespeaking experience too immediate for language: "Can it be that the world is but the great word / That speaks to meaning of our joy?" And at the end the shared experience of the world's beauty counteracts the second of the Three Darknesses, solipsistic isolation. The double use of "contact" here underscores the communion experience typical of Warren's "Osmosis of Being" concept[4]: "Scarcely in consciousness, a hand finds, on stone, a hand. / They are in contact. Past lake, over mountain, last light / Probes for contact with the soft-shadowed land."

Directly in the middle of this collection–Section V of the nine sections–are the poems of boyhood reminiscence mentioned earlier, recalling grandfather, a kindly uncle, an elderly friend of the family, and the poet himself in his Eden period. Immediately thereafter, beginning Section VI, "Muted Music" reduces the faculty of memory to something as fragile as a fly's noise in a barn: "Does the past now cruise your empty skull like / That blundering buzz at barn-height . . .?" (53) But in the end this "muted music" of the past evokes that language beyond words by which the world says something–"the song the moth sings, the babble / Of falling snowflakes (in a language / No school has taught you), the scream / Of the reddening bud of the oak tree / As the bud bursts into the world's brightness." The remaining poems of Section VI–the longest section of *Altitudes and Extensions*–also center upon problems of language and communication. "The

Whole Question" portrays the child's growth into language-speaking as a regression from the reality known to the infant: "You knew more words, but they were words only," so now "you must try to rethink what is real. Perhaps / It is only a matter of language that traps you. You / May yet find a new one in which experience overlaps / Words."

Regarding the "matter of language that traps you," one concept in particular proves most elusive and essential: the search for identity, or self, that brings the solitary seeker beyond the boundary of words and deeply into nature. In "Why Boy Came to Lonely Place," the problem is stated: "You say the name they gave you. That's all you are" (56); in "Platonic Lassitude," immersion in nature frames a solution ("So, lulled, you loll in the lap of Time's wave, and the great crest, / . . . will never descend"), until the crow's call (often a voice of reality in Warren's verse) harshly ends the séance; in "The Place," the self comes closer yet to absorption by nature ("lying on stone, / Among fern fronds, and waiting / For the shadow to find you" [61]); and in "If Snakes Were Blue" (65), the perfect day (with "clouds like pink lily-pads floating") suffices to call back the lost anima with "the kind of promise / We give ourselves in childhood when first dawn / Makes curtains go gold. . . ." Here—tellingly—this recall of the lost anima is connected with the crucial motifs (mentioned earlier from the television screen): "True, few fulfillments—but look! In the distance lift peaks / Of glittering white above the wrath-torn land."

Here in Section VI the immersion in nature is further amplified by a dialectical characterization of the seasons, which are both literal and a figure for the swift passage of a lifetime. In "Seasons," a poem in two parts, the movement from spring to fall evokes the rueful irony featured in Warren's poetry of fifty years ago. Part I, "Downwardness" (58), juxtaposes the "lust for downwardness" in the snow-melt against a tentative "sacred cycle": "But time will change, clouds again draw up buckets, / . . . And in earth-darkness moisture will climb the lattices of clay." Part II, "Interlude of Summer" (59), employs the recurring mountain image in a memorable vignette of time's velocity:

> Evening by evening, the climactic melodrama of
> Day flares from behind the blackening silhouette
> Of the mountain for the last and majestic pyre of
> What of today you can remember, or forget.

Along the way, Warren's favorite flower (symbolizing his Eden period) suffers its own "fall" into a degenerate state: "The woodland violet that was your love is replaced by the roadside aster." And as the lapse accelerates–"The faces of the children are now hardening toward definition," "And gullet has sucked juice from the / . . . tooth-gored pear," "An old friend dies this summer"–the autumn season provokes a strategy of evasion: "But your own health is good. Conversation / Turns to New England foliage, which has begun beautifully. . . . / After all, aesthetics is a branch of philosophy." Yet conversely, "First Moments of Autumn Recognized" (62) celebrates the season, without irony, as pure epiphany:

> . . .From brightest blue
> Spills glitter of afternoon, more champagne than ever
> Summer. Bubble and sparkle burst in
> Tang, taste, tangle, tingle, delicious
> On tongue of spirit, joyful in eye-beam.

This is the sort of beauty that can bring the anima self back from its long exile, "your being perfected / At last, in the instant itself which is unbreathing."

Section VII consists of four more poems about moments of communion without language–through the artistry of music in "Youthful Picnic Long Ago: Sad Ballad on Box" (69-70); through loving touch in "History During Nocturnal Snowfall" (71); through the train's wail in "Whistle of the 3 A.M." (72); and through a shared journey in "Last Night Train" (73-74). Moreover, these poems accentuate the nameless as well as the wordless, suggesting the kind of communion that evokes the anima condition. Whereas names distinguish and separate, namelessness fosters the "Osmosis of Being" process that Warren described in his essay on "Knowledge and the Image of Man." For the sleepers in "History During Nocturnal Snowfall" and "Last Night Train" (involving bedmates and strangers on a train, respectively), the "each alone" status of conscious thought is transcended by "the unconscious wallow of flesh-heap" to which the speaker relates himself in this latter poem. And perhaps the loss of names in "Youthful Picnic Long Ago," including that of the singer ("her name, it flees the fastest!"), finally enhances the "One Life we all live" motif that connects these poems with those of the "Billie Potts" period in the 1940's.

As the pursuit of the lost anima intensifies in Section VIII, the television images observed as tiny and distant in "Three Darknesses" assume imminent proximity. Light and mountains now fill the eye at both the literal and metaphorical level of comprehension. Metaphorically, the light of artistic imagination prevails in "Milton: A Sonnet" (75), restoring to the blind poet something like the anima's joyful presence: "a present in which the blessèd heart / May leap like a gleaming fish from water into / Sunlight. . . ." A similar light of creativity combines with mountain imagery in "Wind and Gibbon," which portrays the great historian's art as a refuge from the night-wind–itself a metaphor of history as chaos: "The wind / Is like a dream of History. Blows where it listeth" (77). Gibbon, of course, elicits design and order from History–"History is not truth. Truth is in the telling" (77). Through the night the "hot lava" of Gibbon's "incandescent irony" lights up the reader's mental landscape like the sun's "single / Beam, sky-arrowing," that "strikes / The mountain to dazzlement" (78) next morning.

The motif of namelessness–correlating with the anima level of identity–continues its prevalence in this penultimate section of *Altitudes and Extensions*. "Whatever You Now Are" (76) asks whether the sleeper who dreams is not a truer self than the conscious ego: "But dawn breaks soon, and that self will have fled away. / Will a more strange one yet inhabit the precinct of day?" And "Sunset" (84)–the penultimate poem in this collection–imposes its ominous setting ("a dire hour") upon the search for "your naked self–never / Before seen, nor known." "Who knows his own name at the last," Warren asks, having vainly "asked stars the name of my soul." Had Warren ended his new collection here, instead of going on to one more poem, the final image behind all those veils may have turned out to be "flaming apocalypse" that consumes identity and all else in this memorable fusion of visual effect and sound-texture:

> Clouds clamber, turgid, the mountain, peakward
> And pine-pierced, toward the
> Vulgar and flaming apocalypse of day,
> In which our errors are consumed
> Like fire in a lint-house–

In the end, the "divine osmosis" threading through these last poems answers the need for identity. In "Delusion?–No!" (79) this merging of self in a collective Being occurs when the mountain-top perspective releases a familiar anima sensibility: "Yes, stretch forth your arms like wings, and from your high stance, / Hawk-eyed, ride forth upon the emptiness of air. . . ." In "Question at Cliff-Thrust" (80-81) this absorption into the world's being occurs in an undersea setting—"one great green . . . depth that steadily / Absorbs your being in its intensity." (In this case it is the bird above the surface that expresses the disconsolation of the separate ego—"once gull that screams . . . and is / Demanding what?") And in "It Is Not Dead" (82-83) the osmosis of being reaches beyond the animate world (where it stopped at the end of "Billie Pots") to embrace equally the inorganic. Like the soul or anima in the animate creation, the rock in the brook "has tried / To find its true nature" since its emergence out of "nameless heat under / Nameless pressure" in the earth's core. Claiming "brotherhood" with this piece of inert matter, and "Brooding on our common destinies," Warren exhibits a pantheism—or at least a vitalism—that recalls Spinoza's dictum that matter thinks. Or, closer to Warren's American heritage, one thinks of Thoreau's vitalistic vision in the "Spring" section of *Walden*: "There is nothing inorganic. . . . The earth is not a mere fragment of dead history . . . but living poetry like the leaves of a tree, which precede flowers and fruit,—not a fossil earth, but a living earth; compared with whose great central life all animal and vegetable life is merely parasitic" (210-211). In Warren's own verse, this strand of vitalism may be traced back through poems like "Interjection #2: Caveat" in *Or Else* (1974), where a fragment of rock "screams / in an ecstasy of / being" (12), all the way to "Kentucky Mountain Farm," where Poem I comprises the "Rebuke of the Rocks" against sexual generation.

Warren's concluding poem, "Myth of Mountain Sunrise" (85), whose eighteen lines are distinctive enough to compose all of Section IX—is a remarkable performance as a culminating expression of Warren's themes and images. The mountain, so tiny and distant in "Three Darknesses," now envelops the observer, immersing him in stone: "No light here enters, has ever entered but / In ageless age of primal flame." Within its "curdling agony of interred dark," however, the mountain's interior thrusts toward daylight—it "strives dayward, in stone strives"—in obedience to the deepest design of nature: "But look! All mountains want slow- / ly to bulge outward extremely." Of course the mountain is animate; more than that, it is personified and humanized as Warren follows its course from night's dream ("Prodigious, prodigal, crags steel-ringing / To dream-hoofs nightlong") to dawn's waking: "The mountain dimly wakes, stretches itself on windlessness. Feels its deepest chasm, waking, yawn." Further, in its own wordless language, the stone speaks—"Words stone-incised in language unknowable, but somehow singing"—as a leaf-tongue verifies by answering the testimony of the stone: "Leaf cries: 'I feel my deepest filament in dark rejoice. / I know that the density of basalt has a voice.'"

The closing six-line stanza of "Myth of Mountain Sunrise" provides a glorious climax of this poem, of this collection, and of Warren's purpose as a poet of youth/rejuvenation. Here the fusion of light and Eros constitutes Warren's wholly original "myth" of sunrise (as he confirmed in a phone conversation with me), yet it bears analogies to both the Semitic "Let there be light" and the Hellenistic Zeus coupling with earthlings. Probably the latter analogy is the more striking for the manly vigor with which the sun's ray grasps by the haunch the birch which stands in the brook, ready to be taken ("head back-flung, eyes closed in first beam"):

> How soon will the spiderweb, dew-dappled, gleam
> In Pompeian glory! Think of a girl-shape, birch-white sapling rising now
> From ankle-deep brook-stones, head back-flung, eyes closed in first beam,
> While hair—long, water-roped, past curve, coign, sway that no geometries
>   know—
> Spreads end-thin, to define fruit-swell of haunches, tingle of hand-hold.
> The sun blazes over the peak. That will be the old tale told.

For "brightness of meaning"—to recall Warren's statement about image in *All the King's Men*—it is difficult to imagine anything more striking than this behind the final veil. What makes it all the more striking is direct contradiction between this closure and those of all Warren's previous volumes of poetry. Up until this volume of his eightieth year, every published collection has ended in an image of full darkness or declining light. To highlight the contrast, it is worth cataloguing those first fourteen closures. In the concluding poem of Warren's first volume, *Thirty-Six Poems* (1935), the father's gravestone "Ascends the night and propagates the dark"; *Eleven Poems on the Same Theme* (1942) moves from "Monologue at Midnight" to

"Terror"; at the end of "The Ballad of Billie Potts" (1943), Little Billie and "you, wanderer" "kneel in the sacramental silence of evening"– "an evening empty of wind or bird"–in acceptance of mortality; *Brother to Dragons* (1953 and 1979) ends with Warrens's meditation "In the last light of December's, and the day's, declension"; *Promises* (1957) ends, in "The Necessity for Belief," with a sunset and moonrise ("The sun is red, and the sky does not scream"); *You, Emperors, and Others* (1960) ends with a set of quatrain poems called "Short Thoughts for Long Nights"; *Tale of Time* (1966) ends, in "Finisterre," with a sunset over San Francisco ("And the last of day, it would seem, goes under"); *Incarnations* (1968) ends with "Fog" ("the luminous blindness"); *Audubon* (1969) ends with "Tell Me A Story," set "By a dirt road, in first dark"); *Or Else* (1974) ends with "A Problem in Spatial Composition," which is a verbal painting of sunset ("Sun now down, flame, above blue, dies upward forever in / Saffron"); *Can I See Arcturus from Where I Stand*? (1975) ends in the late-night setting of "Old Nigger on One-Mule Cart" ("by a bare field, a shack unlit? / Entering into that darkness to fumble / My way to a place to lie down"; *Now and Then* (1978) ends with the poet longing to join the wild geese flying southward "Toward sunset, at a great height"; *Being Here* (1980) ends with "Passers-By on Snowy Night"; *Rumor Verified* (1981) ends with the failing light of "Fear and Trembling" ("The sun now angles downward, and southward"); and even *Chief Joseph of the Nez Perce* ends with the narrator telling his friend, "It's getting night, and a hell of a way / To go."

Theologically, that lusty sun grasping for the world's beauty justifies in the end the pale abstraction in "Three Darknesses," that God loves the world for what it is. We may further postulate that it does something similar for the Spirit of the Deeps, seen wearily receiving the refuse of Time in "Kentucky Mountain Farm." But it is mainly a tribute to the poet's own spirit that in his eightieth year he would so exercise his rejuvenating imagination. A full two decades (and more) ago, George P. Garrett, Jr., compared Warren's "steady growth and blooming" as a poet entering his sixties to "that last astounding harvest of W. B. Yeats" (as well as Picasso and Stravinsky). At that time, Warren had not written half his present poetic *oeuvre*. What can be said now had perhaps best be said by

Warren himself. In a poem in *You, Emperors, and Others* (1960) titled "In the Turpitude of Time: N.D.," Warren wrote: "In the heart's last kingdom only the old are young" (31). Thinking of that paramour sun with his birch lover, we can believe it.

Notes

[1]*Altitudes and Extensions* (1980-1984) is the first section of poems in *New and Selected Poems* (Random 1985) and is viewed by Warren as a new "book" of poems similar to *Can I See Arcturus from Where I Stand?–Poems 1975* (*Selected Poems, 1923-1975*) and *Tale of Time: New Poems, 1960-1966* (*Selected Poems: New & Old, 1923-1966*). [Editor's note.]

[2]Poems cited are from *New and Selected Poems* unless otherwise noted.

[3]Warren's unpublished works are listed, with dates, in *Robert Penn Warren: A Descriptive Bibliography, 1922-1979*, by James A. Grimshaw, Jr. (Charlottesville: UP of Virginia, 1981).

[4]See Warren's essay, first presented as a speech to the American Philological Society, entitled "Knowledge and the Image of Man." It later appeared in *Sewanee Review* 63 (1955): 182-92.

Works Cited

Faulkner, William. "Foreword." *The Faulkner Reader: Selections from the Works of William Faulkner*. New York: Random, 1954.

Garrett, George Palmer, Jr. "The Recent Poetry of Robert Penn Warren." *Robert Penn Warren: A Collection of Critical Essays*. Ed. John L. Longley, Jr. New York: New York UP, 1965. 223-36.

Thoreau, Henry David. *"Walden" and "Civil Disobedience"*. Ed. Sherman Paul. Boston: Houghton, 1960.

Warren, Robert Penn. *All the King's Men*. Modern Library Edition. New York: Random, 1953.

—. *Brother to Dragons: A Tale in Verse and Voices, A New Version*. New York: Random, 1979.

—. *Chief Joseph of the Nez Perce*. New York: Random, 1983.

—. "Knowledge and the Image of Man." *Sewanee Review* 63 (1955): 182-92.

—. *New and Selected Poems, 1923-1985*. New York: Random, 1985.

—. *Or Else–Poem/Poems 1968-1974*. New York: Random, 1974.

—. *Selected Poems: New and Old, 1923-1966*. New York: Random, 1966.

—. *Selected Poems, 1923-1975*. New York: Random, 1975.

—. *You, Emperor, and Others: Poems 1957-1960*. New York: Random, 1960.

THE NONFICTION

Warren and the Narrator as Historical Self

James Justus

It is not surprising that Warren should regard *Snow-Bound* as a signal American achievement. That segment of his introduction to *John Greenleaf Whittier's Poetry* is itself one of the signal achievements of a practical critic whose impact on the way we read poetry has been significant and long-lasting. Warren's is the first reading to stress the fact that this great public poem is also a heroic personal victory over circumstances both cultural and psychological. Rescuing Whittier's poem from last century's pious custodians is in a sense simply one other version of Warren's own struggle with Time, and what this poet identifies as Whittier's strategies and tactics we also see in much of Warren's own work.

Poems set in a personal past are inevitably shaped by a perspective that is both immediate and detached–age recalling and evaluating youth, a double view whose urgency and calculation are greater than what mere nostalgia can provide. Yet Warren identifies Whittier's halting struggle not as abolitionism but as a more personal issue, a sense of loss–how to find "in the contemplation of the past a meaning for the future." With "no landmarks left" after the deaths of his mother and sister, "only memory" could serve to focus that haunting theme (45-46). With his public function discharged at the end of the Civil War, the poet, now past middle age, could continue his exploratory forays into that most baffling territory. As Warren sees it, Whittier's re-creation of an actual world, past and incapable of ordinary retrieval, is an act of inquiry into the complex idea about "the human relation to Time," and the issues most sharply addressed are change, memory, continuity, and personal identity. Even more than for Whittier in his New England meditative epic, Time becomes Warren's great generative theme. Under its aegis are the lyric poems, the historical novels, and the best of the discursive writing on historical subjects.

Warren's friend and colleague, R. W. B. Lewis, once suggested that the basis of Whittier's achievement generally—his method of "interweaving the personal and autobiographical with the national and cultural"—is the same method by which Warren explicates American literature (585).[1] It is also, I think, the method by which Warren explicates American history. The interweaving of biography, philosophy, historical event, and cultural artifact with logical argumentation and speculation—that process that marvelously unifies Warren's separate essays on Melville, Dreiser, Mark Twain, Hawthorne, and Whittier—is no less remarkable in his most distinguished historical essay, *The Legacy of the Civil War.*[2] The best of his historical writing derives from a happy conjunction of factuality and surmise, the first resulting from reading and research, the second from creative imagination.

A professional historian, Thomas L. Connelly, recently admitted that from the academic purist's conception of a historian, Warren would fall short; yet, he gives Warren high marks as historian because he writes from a coherent but flexible philosophy of history and because he so constantly appreciates the impact of past experience upon the present (1-17). The high respect Warren has always shown for the objective record is not that of the documentary historian; but certainly the known facts, many of them nearly lost in the shadowy recesses of court records, memoirs, genealogies, wills, battle narratives, privately published family and local histories, letters and journals, have interested him as deeply and nearly as long as have writing poems and learning how to talk about them. But Warren also knows that factuality is not truth, that meaningful reconstructions of the past require not simply an archivist's diligence but a poet's sensitivity to the interstices of the record. Hence, Warren's first book, *John Brown: The Making of a Martyr* (1929). Authoritative facts must sometimes be enlarged, creatively interpreted, even cautiously extrapolated, by the conscientious searcher. But, more importantly, what we hear in Warren's kind of history is a voice that meditates aloud on the curious shapes that lie waiting to be brought out from among their often inert contexts—shapes that emerge from coincidences, accidents, parallel and overlapping relationships that in turn lay claim to their own patterns of irony and pathos. These shapes are often the result of shrewd surmise. Both factuality and surmise are necessary perspectives that Warren uses in his search for the meaning of an event, which is the ultimate goal of the persona in his kind of history as it is in his kind of fiction and poetry.

The text of *The Legacy of the Civil War* is peppered with dates, thumbnail biographies, battles, names of generals, apt quotations from the famous and peripheral alike—all recorded and waiting to be plucked from the vast shelves of our massive collections of Civil War materials. But it is not Warren's high regard for the objective record that makes *The Legacy of the Civil War* the most impressive revaluation of that corrosive event in the centennial observances twenty years ago. For all the evidence there is never sufficient evidence to satisfy the mind relentlessly in pursuit of the question, *what does it mean*? And so to flesh out the commendable factuality of his meditation Warren unhesitatingly resorts to conjecture, second or third guesses, possible alternatives, implications, all to help satisfy his nagging need to know. By page five of the book Warren has already introduced an anecdote, one of hundreds to come out of Gettysburg, concerning General Pickett's saluting a little girl waving a Federal flag. "'I did not salute the enemy's flag,'" Warren quotes Pickett; "'I saluted the heroic womanhood in the heart of that brave little girl, and the glorious old banner under which I won my first laurels.'" As Warren recognizes, the statement smacks more of family legend than reliable history, but he gives the Confederate general's explanation of his act to reinforce a previous point—that "crypto-unionism" was more common in southern breasts than we have been taught to believe. "True or not," Warren writes, "the tale . . . points to a truth. Shared experiences of the past and shared hopes for the future could not easily be expunged; and I myself have heard an old man who had ridden three years with Forrest, and never regretted that fact, say that he would have sadly regretted the sight of this country 'Balkanized'" (6).

This is a characteristic passage, one which perhaps only Warren could have written. Impersonal anecdotal memory spurs the historian to a generalized truth, followed closely by a ratifying personal memory suggesting the collision of familial loyalties and common-sense: all marshalled in the service of a belief in the complexity and elusiveness of history. The passage signals Warren's pervasive conviction about the force of the past—the influence, for good or ill, of the *done* on the *to be done*. It makes frank use of any apt nugget of information, even though the source may be suspect, if it aesthetically and morally contributes to the meaning of events that he is trying to shape out of the disordered pressures of those events. And finally, as a Warren hallmark, it searches out autobiography as a confirming seal.

The "old man who had ridden three years with Forrest" is, of course, a familiar character in Warren's work. This image–the white-bearded maternal grandfather in jeans, smoking his cob pipe, sitting in a split-bottomed chair propped against a cedar tree, with a small boy sitting at his feet listening to war stories–recurs with such frequency in Warren's poems that it assumes iconographic significance. It is more fully invoked in published interviews. In its special status, it is what we may call one of the enabling images of the artist's past.

If, as Warren believes, the Civil War is our "only 'felt' history–history lived in the national imagination" (4), the role of memory in any direct reassessment of that divisive event must necessarily be slight. (Chronologically, Warren is among the very few now alive who could have known the grandfather who had been in the War.) In *The Legacy of the Civil War* this "felt" perspective is limited to that briefly summoned-up image of the grandfather who had ridden with "the critter company." Though tangential to his larger purpose, the image is an important reminder of the long-lasting effects of that national trauma on several generations in the South; but it is also a tangible example of one of Warren's own great themes–the generative importance of continuities, the shaping of the present by the past. When, however, in the late 1970s Warren had the opportunity to assess the Civil War yet again–this time from a narrower angle, with the focus on a single participant in that struggle–memory could enter the revaluation almost on an equal par with the claims of factuality and surmise. For this reason *Jefferson Davis Gets His Citizenship Back* has an even greater power than *The Legacy of the Civil War*.

The triggering event is contemporary: President Carter's signing of Joint Resolution 16, on October 17, 1978, returning citizenship to Jefferson Davis, the President of the Confederacy who died disenfranchised in 1889, a ceremony which, in turn, inspired a three-day celebration culminating on Davis's birthday the following June 3 in Todd County, Kentucky. The pathetic, pious, sincere, distracted, amateurish nature of public ceremonials in the modern South is documented with all the cruel specificity of Warren, the author of *Flood*. The natural climax of the book, with Warren himself a more-than-casual visitor, comes with the inevitable festivities: a demonstration of old-fashioned soap-making, a gimcrack parade, a formal commemoration with speeches, a square dance, a ball in the high school gym, and a slapdash but earnest staging of an original dramatic musical based on the life and times of Jefferson Davis. The author who attends this homegrown affair of course functions as the point of view, but the present self is persistently modified by memory.

What cannot be forgotten is the self of the past, who is linked with the grandfather, who in turn is linked with the very War in which both the glory and vainglory of Jefferson Davis are remembered. Thus, this image, which had previously functioned as *personal* continuity in the poems "Court-Martial" (from *Promises*), "Safe in Shade" and "When Life Begins" (from *Being Here*) and as a kind of *national* continuity in *The Legacy of the Civil War*, now in *Jefferson Davis* encompasses both the personal and the national. Further, it functions as *formal* continuity, structuring the flow of external event and internal action. The image of the "old man under the cedar tree, meditating on the past while an ignorant little boy sat there tailor-fashion on the ground" begins the Jefferson Davis book, and it recurs twice in the slim volume of 114 pages (1-2). The book is not about Warren's grandfather or about Warren himself as a young boy, but for the first ten pages we are invited to share in a special kind of autobiography—one in which the personal intersects imaginatively with local history, family legend, and the reverberating effects of two wars. Captain Gabriel Penn was 69 and cared for by Warren's youngest aunt when his grandson was born in 1905. From 1911 to 1918 Warren spent most of his childhood summers at his grandfather's place, a Trigg County farm which Warren remembers as being "totally cut off from the rest of the world" (224).[3] This generative period the writer returns to again and again—to himself as a boy, usually nine or twelve, and to the old man who became an "idol" to the boy. He "*was* history," Warren says of Captain Penn in *Jefferson Davis* (9-10). But another history is being enacted in Europe in one of these years of "an unchanging summer." If the grandfather had once been a "crypto-unionist" back in the early 1860s, now in the early

1940s, with an old man's detachment, he can be scornful of the competing claims of small states' rights that could eventuate in war that could "Balkanize" an entire continent.

This moment demonstrates the rhetorical and moral functions of Warren's point of view—the 74-year-old narrator whose perspective includes the willed re-creation of himself at nine, ten, eleven, and twelve. The boy's confusion in "the matter of Jefferson Davis" seems at first merely a matter of his innocence and ignorance. The name does not have the same meaning to him as it does to his grandfather; to the boy the referent is someone known locally as Old Jeff Davis, a feckless handyman, talentless, poor, and odorous, who with Mrs. Jeff trudges to town along the railroad track with a croker-sack to bring home the week's "traden." The mature narrator can add that this old man was "a walking monument to Jefferson Davis" years before the great monolith honoring the Confederate president went up a few miles to the north of his home town, so that similarities between the two Davises are insinuated back into the account. The boy's rhetorical question—"The world-shaker dwindled to this?"—is implicitly affirmed by the general outline of the Jefferson Davis story already known by adults, an almost quintessential story of dwindling—of national and personal failure, of humiliation after momentary and controversial fame. "Bit by bit," says the narrator, "things sorted themselves out, and the deficiencies of the world-shaker began to have some documentation." If the deficiencies of Old Jeff—ineradicably locked into his social and economic position as "lowest of the low"—are contained and localized, perhaps even harmless, those of the world-shaker are damaging both individually and nationally. And if Old Jeff can do nothing about his character and fate, so the real Jefferson Davis cannot change his. With all his learning, devotion to principle, logic, and his reputation for honor and heroism, the world-shaker can never compromise, can never turn himself into a political animal. "Davis was what he was, and he was caught in the complications of the world he lived in . . ." (61). So through the confusing identities of a young boy come the meaningful, human parallels of the historian-artist.

But the radiating ironies are not over. At the end of the account, the 74-year-old native returns to his county, not only to visit anew the nearby concrete obelisk honoring the revered President of the

Confederacy but also to locate the grave markers of Old Jeff and Mrs. Jeff. The crudities and half-hearted pieties involved in the construction of the Jefferson Davis memorial are repeated, in little, in the crude, home-crafted, box-like cement marker made by Old Jeff himself for his wife when she died in 1941; and the "grateful country" which honors its leaders by such visible monuments as the shaft at Fairview also honors its followers: it turns out that Old Jeff had been a Spanish-American War veteran and had thus earned the government marker placed on his grave.

The parallels between the two Davises, however, are never forced; they are not reduced to witty juxtapositions or made to yield bemused ironies at the expense of either objective record or personal memory—as they might have in hands of that younger amateur historian who once wrote about John Brown. Perhaps a more telling parallel is that between substance and rhetoric, between subject and author; for I would suggest that the primary creation in this account is neither of the two Davises but rather a moral persona who in his drive to extract meaning from event is heavily committed to the affirmation of the *merely human.* The shifting interchange between the twelve-year-old character and the 74-year-old narrator produces, in effect, a historical self, much like that wished-for sensibility Warren once proposed. In *The Legacy of the Civil War* he asked for the ability that, without special justifications, would "see the problems and values" of a recreated moment of the past "and those of our own, set against each other in mutual criticism and clarification" (99). If history is unable to "give us a program for the future," he wrote in 1961, it can give us "a fuller understanding of ourselves, and of our common humanity, so that we can better face the future" (100).

The story of Jefferson Davis is of an "unself-conscious Southerner" from Kentucky who is gradually transformed through association, study, and occupation into a conventional Southerner from Mississippi. The story of the narrator is of a twelve-year-old Kentuckian, distinguished only by an "early brand of uninstructed Southernism," who grows into a 74-year-old distinguished observer of things both Southern and American. Although in Davis's growth a certain yeoman virtue is suppressed by a planter-and-slaveholder morality, the narrator insists upon the consistent human rectitude of the world-shaker; in both his glory and his humiliation this is the trait that redeems–and redeems both the person who endures his lot and the person who meditates upon that spectacle. Out of the growth of the narrator from a character of "ignorance" and "uninstructed Southernism" emerges a historical self capable of mutual criticism and clarification. Standing out from the often tawdry and always sad diminution of Davis's public reputation is what Warren calls the "irrefrangible personal identity" of one who both suffers and triumphs. And with the firmness of that identity established for his and our contemplation, Warren speculates on the larger irony involved in having citizenship thrust upon "old-fashioned" men like Robert E. Lee and Jefferson Davis by a newfangled nation "technologically and philosophically devoted to the depersonalization of men" (113). Beyond the formal demands of a persona, this is the voice of a historical self.

Factuality, *surmise*, *memory*: the associative mingling of these necessary perspectives accounts for the best of Warren's historical writing; but only the moral function of memory, the measuring of present against past to locate not merely the meaning of event but "the human relation to Time" itself, can account for the peculiarly resonant accomplishment of *Jefferson Davis Gets His Citizenship Back*. What we hear in this voice is, I think, what we hear in the later volumes of Warren's poetry, especially in *Being Here*, that other book that coincided with the author's 75th birthday–the urgency and continuing humility of the poet-as-searcher. In the later poems there is scarcely a trace of what we conventionally call "wisdom," and certainly little of the complacency that often accompanies the work of the old poet. In his volumes of the last decade Warren plumbs the possibilities for wisdom in both the *now* and the *then*, but his characteristic sentence is interrogative rather than declarative:

> Indeed, what exists in the grab-bag of pastness?
> Do all things, in that vatic darkness, wear
> Two faces? And frozen in hope–or despair–
> Do you guess what may arise from that dark, seething vastness
>
> That was your life? (*Rumor Verified* 87)[4]

If in *Being Here* the thematic motif–what we might summarize as Identity in Time–plays against the structure of what Warren calls a "shadowy autobiography," a similar process is enacted in *Jefferson*

Davis.

Despite the erosions of Time, the treacheries of the Self, or the ambiguities and paradoxes of our history, what we still hear is the persistence of the merely human. What is remarkable in the personae of both the later poems and *Jefferson Davis* is the absence of despair. Exclamations of joy coexist with the night-sweats. To assert the merely human is not to succumb to mere resignation. Warren himself enacts the process of victory he claimed for Whittier, who "came to see that man's fate is that he must learn to accept and use his past completely, knowingly, rather than to permit himself to be used, ignorantly, by it" (*Whittier* 56).

Notes

[1]Lewis also collaborated with Warren and Cleanth Brooks in editing *American Literature: The Makers and the Making* (New York: St. Martin's, 1973).

[2]The literary essays, stimulated by his preparation for the Brooks-Lewis-Warren anthology, are the introductions in *Selected Poems of Herman Melville: A Reader's Edition* and *Homage to Theodore Dreiser*, the Twain essay in *Southern Review*, and the Hawthorne essay in *Sewanee Review*.

[3]See similar remarks throughout this volume of collected interviews.

[4]From the poem, "If Ever." I have discussed the later poetry in some detail in "Warren's Later Poetry: Unverified Rumors of Wisdom," *Mississippi Quarterly* 37 (1984): 161-71.

Works Cited

Connelly, Thomas L. "Robert Penn Warren as Historian." *A Southern Renascence Man: Views of Robert Penn Warren*. Ed. Walter B. Edgar. Baton Rouge: Louisiana State UP, 1984.

Lewis, R. W. B. "Warren's Long Visit to American Literature." *Yale Review* 70 (1981): 568-91.

Stitt, Peter. "An Interview with Robert Penn Warren." *Robert Penn Warren Talking: Interviews 1950-1978*. Ed. Floyd C. Watkins and John T. Hiers. New York: Random, 1980.

Warren, Robert Penn. "Hawthorne Revisited." *Sewanee Review* 81 (1973): 75-111.

—. *Homage to Theodore Dreiser, August 27, 1871-December 28, 1945, on the Centennial of His Birth.* New York: Random, 1971.

—. *Jefferson Davis Gets His Citizenship Back.* Lexington: UP of Kentucky, 1980.

—. *John Greenleaf Whittier's Poetry: An Appraisal and a Selection.* Minneapolis: U of Minnesota P, 1971.

—. *The Legacy of the Civil War: Meditations on the Centennial.* New York: Random, 1961.

—. "Mark Twain." *Southern Review* ns 8 (1972): 459-92.

—. *Rumor Verified: Poems 1979-1980.* New York: Random, 1981.

—. *Selected Poems of Herman Melville: A Reader's Edition.* New York: Random, 1970.

Bibliographical Note

Warren's continued popularity and recognition as one of the leading men of letters in the United States are best illustrated, perhaps, by the amount of attention paid him in this decade. Besides the distinction of being appointed as the first U. S. Poet Laureate in the spring of 1986, Warren's reputation has been sustained by the publication of various new and special editions of his works, by the number of books issued about his work, and by the growing number of individual scholarly articles which pertain to his writings.

Although this brief note does not attempt to list everything that has appeared by and about Warren since 1980, it does provide a sampling of those titles which might be of interest to the users of this volume; and in doing so, it provides yet another index to his continuing contribution to American literature.

New Editions and Writings

At Heaven's Gate (Harcourt, 1943) has been reissued by New Directions Books (1985) in paperback, making available Warren's second novel in an inexpensive edition once again. Four other works have also been published in new paperbacks: *All the King's Men* (Harcourt, 1946) appeared in 1982 in two versions of the Harcourt Brace Jovanovich Harvest/HBJ edition. One is in small (10 1/2-pt.) type, and the other in enlarged (12-pt.) type. Also published as a Harvest/HBJ edition is *The Circus in the Attic and Other Stories* in 1983. Warren's last novel, *A Place to Come To* (Random, 1977), has recently been reissued as a Laurel paperback by Dell in 1986. And Harvard University Press published *The Legacy of the Civil War* (Random, 1961) in paperback in 1983. These paperback editions will be particularly welcomed for classroom use.

Four new volumes of poetry by Warren have appeared since 1980: *Being Here: Poetry 1977-1980* (1980), *Rumor Verified: Poems 1979-1980* (1981), *Chief Joseph of the Nez Perce* (1983), and *New and Selected Poems, 1923-1985* (1985). Each title was issued by Random

House in trade hardcover, in paperback, and in a limited, signed edition. Two of those books were advertised initially under different titles: *Being Here* as "Life Is a Fable" and *Rumor Verified* as "Have You Ever Eaten Stars?" Also appearing for the first time was *Jefferson Davis Gets His Citizenship Back* (UP of Kentucky, 1980).

For collectors, several new editions have been printed. An edition of *All the King's Men* commemorating the thirty-fifth anniversary of that novel's publication was released in 1981 by Harcourt; it contains illustrations by Warren Chappell and a new introduction by Warren. And in 1983 the International Collectors Library (Garden City) printed *All the King's Men*, a facsimile of the more expensive Franklin Library editions and without illustrations. The Franklin Library issued Warren's *New and Selected Poems, 1923-1985* in 1985 in the series, The Signed First Edition Society; this limited edition is not the same as the limited, signed edition issued at time of publication by Random House.

From private and other special-edition presses have come the following books and broadsides: *Ballad of a Sweet Dream of Peace: A Charade for Easter* (Dallas: New London Press, 1980), illustrated by Bill Komodore; from the Palaemon Press in Winston-Salem, NC, *Love: Four Versions* (1981), "Mountain Mystery" (broadsheet, 1981), and *Robert Penn Warren: 15 Poems* (1985); "Rebuke of the Rocks" (broadsheet, 1985) by the Press at Colorado College; and "New Dawn: Hiroshima" in John Hersey's *Hiroshima* (New York: Limited Editions Club, 1983), illustrated by Jacob Lawrence.

Among the many works which Warren has written and edited with others, *Short Story Masterpieces* (with Albert Erskine) was reprinted as a Laurel edition by Dell in 1986.

Shorter nonfiction which Warren published during this period includes "John O'Hara's Short Stories," a memoir, in the *John O'Hara Journal* (1980); "In the Time of *All the King's Men*," *New York Times Book Review* (31 May 1981); introductions to *The Collected Stories of Caroline Gordon* (1981), Brainard Cheney's 1942 novel *River Rogue* (reprinted 1982), William Ferris's *Local Color: A Sense of Place in Folk Art* (1982), the Foreword to *Robert Penn Warren: A Descriptive Bibliography* (1982), Elizabeth Madox Roberts's *The Time of Man: A Novel* (reprinted 1982), *The Collected Stories of Conrad Aiken* (1982); a headnote to Otis C. Williams, Jr.'s "For Your Future Reference" in the *Georgia Review* (1981); "John Crowe Ransom: The First Poet I Ever Saw," in the *New York Times Book Review* (20 May 1984); and "Poetry Is a Kind of Unconscious Autobiography," in the *New York Times Book Review* (12 May 1985).

New Books about Warren

Fifteen new books dealing solely with Warren's works have been published since 1980, a number which increases by 70% the previous number available. Among those fifteen, two are reissues, one is a bibliography, four are full-length studies, and eight are collections of essays.

The two revisions of previously published titles include Charles Bohner's *Robert Penn Warren* (1981) in the Twayne series, a study still useful as an introduction to Warren's work, and a new Cliffs Notes on *All the King's Men* (1982).

James A. Grimshaw, Jr.'s *Robert Penn Warren: A Descriptive Bibliography, 1922-1979* was published in 1982 and offers for the first time a listing of Warren's manuscripts and the printing history of his publications. Since the publication of that bibliography, Yale University has purchased the Warren deposit in the Beinecke Rare Book and Manuscript Library, the location of many of the items described and cataloged in Grimshaw's bibliography.

Among the four full-length studies, only one attempts to deal with the entire Warren canon. James Justus's *The Achievement of Robert Penn Warren* (1981), part of the Southern Literary Series (LSU), exceeds expectations in Warren scholarship and is clearly the best single work published to date. *Then & Now: The Personal Past in the Poetry of Robert Penn Warren* (1982), by Floyd C. Watkins, provides some interesting glimpses into Warren's life, glimpses obtained primarily from public documents, gleaned from careful reading of the texts, and gathered from interviews both published and unpublished. While useful in the absence of an authorized biography, its accuracy remains to be seen. In 1983 Katherine Snipes's *Robert Penn Warren* appeared in the Ungar Literature and Life series. Dealing with the novels and to a lesser extent with the poetry, Snipes offers few new insights to Warren's works. On the other hand, Calvin Bedient's 1984 book, *"In the Heart's Last Kingdom": Robert Penn Warren's Major*

Poetry, provides an interesting contrast to Victor Strandberg's two books on Warren's poetry and deals with the major characteristics of Warren's poetry.

The eight collections of essays include a most useful collection of published interviews, *Robert Penn Warren Talking: Interviews 1950-1978* (1980), edited by Floyd C. Watkins and John T. Hiers. Warren is a conversationalist, and this record of his "talking" captures that ability well. Thomas L. Connelly's *A Southern Renascence Man: Views of Robert Penn Warren* (1984) is the outgrowth of a 1982 Institute for Southern Studies program sponsored by the University of South Carolina. Another product, in part, of a program dedicated to Robert Penn Warren's work is James A. Grimshaw, Jr.'s book, *Robert Penn Warren's "Brother to Dragons": A Discussion* (1983). Four of the essays included appear in print for the first time after they were presented at a special Modern Language Association session in 1979. A small volume of five essays, only one of which had been published previously, is *Homage to Robert Penn Warren*, edited by Frank Graziano in 1981. The charming poem by Rosanna Warren accents the emphasis of the essays on her father's poetry. The other four volumes, primarily reprints of previously published essays, are Richard Gray's *Robert Penn Warren: A Collection of Critical Essays* (1980), in the Prentice-Hall Twentieth-Century Views series; *Robert Penn Warren: Critical Perspectives* (1981) by Neil Nakadate; *Critical Essays on Robert Penn Warren* (1981), edited by William Bedford Clark for the G. K. Hall series; and the Modern Critical Views series *Robert Penn Warren* (1986), edited by Harold Bloom.

Other Secondary Material about Warren

Some books which devote sections or chapters to Warren's works are Thomas Daniel Young's *The Past in the Present: A Study of Modern Southern Fiction* (1981) and *Waking Their Neighbors Up: The Nashville Agrarians Rediscovered* (1982); Louis D. Rubin, Jr.'s *A Gallery of Southerners* (1982) and *The History of Southern Literature* (1985), for which he served as general editor; Lewis P. Simpson's essay, "The Fable of the Writer in Southern Fiction," in *Prospects: The Annual of American Cultural Studies* (1982), edited by Jack Salzman; *The Fugitives, the Agrarians and Other Twentieth-Century*

Southern Writers, edited by Joan St. C. Crane in 1985; and a long-awaited book by Peter Stitt, *The World's Hieroglyphic Beauty: Five American Poets* (1985). A charming coffee-table book which includes a photograph and biographical sketch of Warren is Mark Morrow's *Images of the Southern Writer* (1985).

During the 1980s numerous celebrations involving Warren occurred. In October 1980 the University of Kentucky sponsored the Robert Penn Warren 75th Birthday Symposium. Many of the papers presented at that symposium appeared in *The Kentucky Review* (1981). Following the Kentucky meeting was a reunion of the Agrarians at Vanderbilt University, the proceedings from which were edited by William C. Havard and Walter Sullivan, *A Band of Prophets: The Vanderbilt Agrarians after Fifty Years* (1982). Two commemorations of the *Southern Review* were produced at LSU: in 1980, *"The Southern Review," Original Series, 1935-1942: A Commemoration*, with a "Preface" by Lewis P. Simpson; and in October 1985 a Southern Letters & Modern Literature National Literary Conference, which marked the 50th year since the establishment of the Original Series of the *Southern Review*. A publication of the papers at that conference is planned by the LSU Press.

Among the dozens of articles published in scholarly journals and conveniently cataloged in the *MLA Annual Bibliography* and the *MHRA Annual Bibliography* are these representative selections: Robert B. Heilman, "Baton Rouge and LSU Forty Years After," *Sewanee Review* (1980); Glen M. Johnson, "The Pastness of *All the King's Men*," *American Literature* (1980); James E. Rocks, "Warren's 'Blackberry Winter': A Reading," *University of Mississippi Studies in English* (1980); Victor Strandberg, "Warren's Poetic Vision: A Reading of *Now and Then*," *Southern Review* (1980); Robert Davis Murray, "*Brideshead Revisited* and *All the King's Men*: Towards a Definition of Forties Sensibility," *Evelyn Waugh Newsletter* (1980); Allen Shepherd, "Robert Penn Warren the Novelist, Now (and Then)," *Southern Literary Journal* (1980); Albert E. Wilheim, "Images of Initiation in Robert Penn Warren's 'Blackberry Winter,'" *Studies in Short Fiction* (1980); Leonard Casper, "Circle with a Center Outside: Robert Penn Warren's *A Place to Come To*," *Sewanee Review* (1980); T. R. Hummer, "Robert Penn Warren: *Audubon* and the Moral Center," *Southern Review* (1980); Cleanth Brooks, "Episode and Anecdote in the Poetry of

Robert Penn Warren," *Yale Review* (1981); Malcolm Cowley, "Robert Penn Warren at 75," *Georgia Review* (1981); Richard Jackson, "The Generous Time: Robert Penn Warren and the Phenomenology of the Moment," *Boundary 2* (1981); Richard G. Law, "*At Heaven's Gate*: 'The Fires of Irony,'" (1981); R. W. B. Lewis, "Warren's Long Visit to American Literature," *Yale Review* (1981); Max A. Webb, "*Audubon*: Robert Penn Warren's Response to Eudora Welty's 'A Still Moment,' " *Mississippi Quarterly* (1981); William Bedford Clark, "Warren's *Audubon*: The Artist as Hero," *South Atlantic Quarterly* (1982); Norton R. Girault, "Recollections of Robert Penn Warren as Teacher in the 1930's," *Texas Writers Newsletter* (1982); Susan V. Donaldson, "'Let That Anvil Ring': Robert Penn Warren's *The Cave* and Hawthorne's Legacy," *Southern Literary Journal* (1983); and the spring 1984 issue of the *Mississippi Quarterly*, devoted to articles about Robert Penn Warren. . . .

The list continues, of course, and the readings of Warren's works are becoming more detailed; Warren's own breadth, more acknowledged; and the interrelatedness of his works among themselves and among the works of others, more appreciated. If a discernible trend in the 1980s criticism exists (and it may be too early to tell), it seems to have two emphases: on the one hand, a closer analysis of Warren's narrative technique, poetics, and style, and on the other, a probing of the autobiographical elements within his writings. Those concerns, and topics not yet discovered, will surely be addressed after scholars gain access to the 17,000-plus letters, to the manuscripts, and to the source materials now being added to the permanent collection of the Beinecke Rare Book and Manuscript Library at Yale University.

JAGJr

Contributors

FRANCES BIXLER has written articles entitled "Anne Sexton's *The Awful Rowing Toward God* and the Northern Romantic Painters," "Links Between Chaucer's 'Pardoner's Tale' and the 'Second Nun's Tale,'" and "Richard Wilbur: 'Hard as Nails.'" Currently, she is working on a critical analysis of Robert Penn Warren's *Meet Me in the Green Glen.*

LEONARD CASPER, Boston College professor and author of *Robert Penn Warren: The Dark and Bloody Ground* (1960), is working on a book about Warren's novels since *The Cave.* He has also published a collection of stories, *A Lion Unannounced* (National Council on the Arts, 1970), and six books on the Philippines.

WILLIAM BEDFORD CLARK is Associate Professor of English at Texas A&M University and editor of the *South Central Review.* His essays and articles on Warren have appeared in *American Literature*, the *South Atlantic Quarterly*, and the *Kenyon Review.* He edited the volume on Warren in the G. K. Hall Critical Essays on American Literature series.

JAMES A. GRIMSHAW, JR., Professor and Head, Department of Literature and Languages, East Texas State University, has published *Robert Penn Warren: A Descriptive Bibliography* (Virginia UP), *Robert Penn Warren's "Brother to Dragons": A Discussion* (LSU Press), and *The Flannery O'Connor Companion* (Greenwood).

JAMES H. JUSTUS, Professor of English at Indiana University since 1969, is the author of *The Achievement of Robert Penn Warren* (1981) and numerous essays on Warren, Faulkner, the Fugitive-Agrarians, and other writers of the Southern Renascence. He is currently at work on a critical study of antebellum southern humor.

Contributors

RICHARD G. LAW, Associate Professor and Associate Dean of the College of Sciences and Arts, Washington State University, has published work on the Nashville group in *American Literature*, *Journal of Southern Literature*, and *Studies in the Novel*.

RANDOLPH RUNYON, who was born in Maysville, Kentucky, teaches American Studies and French at Miami University, Oxford, Ohio. He has published on Warren's fiction in the *Southern Literary Journal* and the *Mississippi Quarterly*. He is the author as well of *Fowles/Irving/Barthes: Canonical Variations on an Apocryphal Theme* (Ohio State UP, 1981).

VICTOR STRANDBERG has been a member of the English Department at Duke University since 1966. His most recent books are *The Poetic Vision of Robert Penn Warren*, *A Faulkner Overview: Six Perspectives*, and *Religious Psychology in American Literature: A Study in the Relevance of William James*.